Helping English Language Learners Meet the Common Core

Assessment and Instructional Strategies, K–12

Paul Boyd-Batstone

Routledge
Taylor & Francis Group
New York London

First published 2013 by Eye On Education

Published 2013 by Routledge
711 Third Avenue, New York, NY 10017, USA
2 Park Square, Milton Park, Abingdon, Oxon OX14 4RN

Routledge is an imprint of the Taylor & Francis Group, an informa business

Photo credits:
Figure 7.1 Memo Angeles/Shutterstock.com
Figure 4.1: mtkang/Shutterstock.com
Figure 4.2: Juriah Mosin/Shutterstock.com
Figure 4.9: Leremy, mikiekwoods, puruan, SoleilC, phipatbig, and Pixel Embargo/Shutterstock.com
Figure 7.11: Helder Almeida/Shutterstock.com

Library of Congress Cataloging-in-Publication Data

Boyd-Batstone, Paul.
Helping English language learners meet the common core : assessment and instructional strategies, K–12 / Paul Boyd-Batstone.
      pages   cm
Includes bibliographical references.
ISBN 978-1-59667-237-6
1. English language--Study and teaching--Foreign speakers.
2. Educational tests and measurements.
I. Title.
PE1128.A2B654 2013
428.0071—dc23   2012049455

Cover Designer: Dave Strauss, 3FoldDesign

ISBN: 978-1-596-67237-6 (pbk)

About the Author

Paul Boyd-Batstone, Ph.D. is a professor and chair of the Department of Teacher Education at California State University, Long Beach. He has worked for more than 25 years with diverse student populations and teacher development at all levels. His experience extends from Spanish bilingual education to Cambodian, Khmer/English, literacy development.

He is the author of a number of books on English language development, early literacy for English language learners, classroom assessment, and the theoretical intersection of language acquisition and reader response. He is delighted to author this book with Eye On Education on meeting the needs of ELLs in a Common Core State Standards context.

His service to the field included working on the International Reading Association's Language Diversity Committee and chairing the International Reading Association's Commission on Second Language Literacy and Learning. This work has opened up opportunities to conduct teacher development and literacy work in Guatemalan schools.

Acknowledgments

My first encounter with Eye On Education happened at a conference, not too long ago, when I had the good fortune to cross paths with Dan Sickles, Vice President of Eye On Education. I deeply appreciated his interest in serving the needs of busy teachers with quality ways to teach all students. Our conversation spurred me to send him a proposal for this book idea on English language learner quick assessment in a Common Core context. I was surprised when his father, Robert "Bob" Sickles, President of Eye On Education, responded to me the same day he received the proposal! In subsequent discussions about the book development, Bob promised me that I would work with an experienced editor, and he was more than true to his word. Lauren Davis, Senior Editor has been remarkably responsive and insightful throughout the entire development of the book. She knows the field, she knows books, understands layout and design. In short, she has been the best editor I have ever had the pleasure to work with. I can't thank the entire staff at Eye On Education enough.

One other special acknowledgement is of my daughter, Kathryn Boyd-Batstone. She provided a photograph, used in Chapter 3, of a friend kicking a soccer ball in front of a misty forest in Florence, Oregon. She is a gifted photographer majoring in photojournalism at the University of Oregon. I can't help it; I'm a proud daddy. You can view her stunning photographs at www .kathrynboydbatstone.com.

This book is dedicated to
Dr. Carole Cox,
a true mentor in all ways.

She communicates the legacy of Rosenblatt
in her published works and classroom instruction.

Supplemental Downloads

Many of the tools discussed and displayed in this book are also available on the Routledge website as Adobe Acrobat files. Permission has been granted to purchasers of this book to download these tools and print them.

You can access these downloads by visiting www.routledge.com/9781596672376 and click on the Free Downloads tab.

Contents

Part 1

The Classroom Assessment of Language Levels

1

Introduction and Overview of the Classroom Assessment of Language Levels

This book presents the Classroom Assessment of Language Levels (CALL). It was designed for busy teachers looking to help English language learners (ELLs) meet the demands of the Common Core Listening and Speaking Standards with appropriate instructional strategies tied to language levels. The CALL is a single page grid of essential information for language assessment and instruction across language levels. In just a few moments of interview or small-group interactions, a teacher can make a reliably accurate judgment of an ELL's instructional needs. The language levels are matched to appropriate instructional strategies that have wide application across grade levels. Because language proficiency is not directly tied to a specific grade level, the assessment tool can be used across grade levels, K–12, with adjustments for degree of content. This book also addresses an in-depth discussion of appropriate ways to address each Common Core Listening and Speaking Standard within the grade level ranges of kindergarten–grade 2, grades 3–5, grades 6–8, and grades 9–10 and 11–12 for English language learners at the beginning, early intermediate, intermediate, early advanced, and advanced stages of language proficiency.

Addressing classroom assessment for English language learners, Common Core Standards, and grade level instructional strategies for K–12 is like playing a game of three-dimensional chess. Because this is an initial book on the CALL, the authors and editors made some organizational decisions to keep the scope of the book to a manageable level. The first part of the book, chapters 1–3, provides an overview and procedures regarding the CALL. The second part of the book, chapters 4–8, provides an in-depth look at each language level and ways to address each Common Core Listening and Speaking Standard for grades K–12. We decided to narrow the Common Core to the Listening and Speaking Standards because instruction with English language learners begins with listening and speaking. I hope to address each domain of the Common Core Standards in relation to differentiated instruction for English language learners in future publications.

This chapter addresses the following:

+ Why is another assessment tool necessary?
+ Background for the CALL
+ Assessment for English language development
+ What is the CALL?
+ Who will use this assessment tool?
+ What is in this book?

Why Is Another Assessment Tool Necessary?

Picture the following scenario: you are a classroom teacher, and your instructional day is in progress. In the middle of a lesson, someone knocks on the door. It is the school counselor accompanying a new student to your room. Because you work in a diverse setting, you are not surprised that the student is an English language learner. However, you have very little information about the student, and you don't have the luxury of waiting several months for the arrival of the results of standardized tests. Time is not on the child's side. You need a quick assessment of the student's English language level so that you can begin effective instruction immediately. This calls for a formative assessment tool for identifying language level and appropriate accommodations quickly. It is time for the CALL.

Background for the CALL

Classroom teachers at all levels, K–12, face the above challenge on a daily basis. Valdez & Callahan (2011) noted that 20 percent of the U.S. population five years and older was reported as speaking more than one language, according to the Federal Interagency Forum (2009). Additionally, between 1970 and 2000, the number of specific language groups in the United States grew dramatically, specifically Spanish and Asian languages, such as Vietnamese, Khmer, and Korean. Those numbers are even higher in urban settings. What this means is that all classroom teachers across the country can expect to be responsible to teach students whose first language is other than English.

Another important point in teaching English language learners is that multiple factors are involved (August & Shanahan, 2007). Language level, for instance, is not tied to grade level. Although this may sound obvious at first, consider the complexities for instruction. Two English language learners can arrive at a fourth grade classroom at the same time. One may have had instruction in English and have lived in the country for a number of years; the other may be a newly arrived immigrant with a very limited knowledge of English. Where to begin instruction with either English learner requires a quick formative assessment to inform instruction.

In this case, summative assessments are not helpful. Summative assessments provide "after-the-fact summaries of learning" (Afflerbach & Clark, 2011, p. 307). They focus on products of learning and achievement of processes and are typically conducted at the end of a unit of study. They may also involve large populations of students for generalizing results and establishing trends. In contrast, formative assessment, according to Sadler (1989), provides teachers with information about individual students, not large populations. The information provided is about the progress as a learner. In other words, teachers use formative assessment to know how to accommodate learning, revise instruction, and shape instruction to the specific needs of the learner. The Classroom Assessment of Language Levels is a formative assessment tool.

According to Afflerbach & Clark (2011), the purposes of assessment vary according to the diverse needs of its audiences. Students need to build independence as learners, teachers need to inform their instruction, parents need to understand their children's achievement, administrators need to determine a program's effectiveness, politicians need to determine accountability for funding, and taxpayers need to know that their money is well spent. No single assessment can address all those needs. This CALL is designed specifically for the needs of the classroom teacher. It may help teach children what they need to do to become more-effective students. It may help parents understand what language levels their children are evidencing. But it is primarily intended to inform instruction. Consequently, it will not address program improvement, accountability, or funding issues.

The primary purpose of the CALL is to give classroom teachers an easy-to-use, formative assessment tool to quickly identify a student's language level. It also provides differentiated questioning techniques and strategies at a glance to match instruction to the student's level. The emphasis is on quick assessment for selecting appropriate instructional accommodations. (Disclaimer: The CALL is not designed to supplant any current state or district level assessment of English language learners for formal identification or redesignation purposes.)

Assessment for English Language Development

The impetus for developing formal assessment of English language learners came from the No Child Left Behind (NCLB, 2001) legislation. Foundationally, various researchers (Sato, Lagunoff, Worth, Bailey, and Butler, 2005; Butler, Lord, Stevens, Borrego, & Bailey, 2003–2004) established a link between academic achievement and applied linguistics. This provided the basis for the development of English Language Development measures that are used statewide, such as the California English Language Development Test (CELDT) (Murphy, Bailey, and Butler, 2006). The exam assesses both the linguistic features (phonological, lexical, and syntactic) and academic language functions (discourse) commonly used in K–12 schooling. It may take as long as 45 minutes to administer to a single student and provides a language level score but does not specify instruction. Further, the lag time between assessment and receiving the results can be anywhere from four to eight months, which further removes the assessment from instruction.

As stipulated by NCLB (2001) legislation, ELD assessment is required to align with academic content standards. There are ongoing attempts to develop Content Standards for English Language Development such as the CSELD (Sacramento, 1999) and the recent efforts at Stanford University headed up by Dr. Kenji Hakuta (www.stanford.edu). The grade range framework and stages of language proficiency provided the organizational foundation for the CALL. Language level and grade level are not the same. For example, a fourth-grade student and a tenth-grade student could be assessed at the same intermediate level of language proficiency.

What Is the CALL?

I organized the CALL tool into a seven-column table that includes the following headings that are essential to language assessment: level, stages, duration, questions, interactive techniques, student behaviors, differentiated strategies. The heading terminology is defined as follows:

◆ *Levels:* The levels are numbered 1 to 5 with 5 being the highest or nearest to fully fluent level. The application of five levels is in line with other assessment formats for English Language Learners such as WIDA (2012) and TESOL (2010).

◆ *Stages:* The five corresponding stages use the following descriptors: (1) beginning, (2) early intermediate, (3) intermediate, (4) early advanced, and (5) advanced. I understand that lockstep stages are an abstraction of the reality of language development. Language is developed more in phases that overlap and even reoccur in new situations. WIDA and TESOL use the term "descriptors" to show a progression of language development. Their descriptors are similar in name and somewhat metaphorical in style. For example, WIDA calls their beginning level descriptor "Entering," whereas TESOL refers to it as "Starting." The other four descriptors are identical as follows: Emerging, Developing, Expanding, and Bridging. Although I appreciate the richness of the metaphorical language, the continuum of descriptors is not readily apparent. I could see it being very easy to confuse "Entering" and "Emerging" because the words mean virtually the same thing outside of this context. Therefore, I chose to use more graded descriptors (beginning through advanced) to clearly show a continuum and to reduce confusion.

◆ *Duration:* Using the work of Collier and Thomas (1987), I aligned the levels and stages with the duration, in months to years, one could reasonably expect a student to remain given that no other factors impeded language development.

◆ *Questioning/Interactive Techniques:* I created a column for questioning and interactive techniques for two reasons. The differentiated questioning techniques initiate a conversation for assessment; they are also used with interactive techniques and strategies at a glance. Questions are the invitation for interaction; however, certain types of questions are more appropriate for students at earlier stages. The questions need to be tailored to the students' stages of language development. Specifically, students at the earliest stages of language development can respond with only a limited set of gestures and words. Asking students at that stage to describe their thoughts at length would most likely result in blank stares. Using differentiated questions during the assessment facilitates the process, giving students a way to respond according to a particular stage of language development.

Questioning and interactive techniques also work hand in glove with instructional strategies. For example, if a teacher displays real objects, realia, to teach new vocabulary, the types of questions used in the instruction may change according to the level of the student. A level 1 student at the beginning stage of development will not be able to answer a question about the realia unless it is framed as yes or no—"Is this a banana?"— or either/or—"Is this a banana or is it an apple?" Asking a student at that level to respond to an open-ended question—such as "What do you know about bananas?"—would be a waste of time given the ability of the student to respond. Initially, I combined the questions and interactive techniques, but I realized that questions worked best in direct interview settings, and interactive techniques facilitate observations in small-group instructional settings. Middle- and high-school teachers, who work with as many as 200 or more students each day, might find conducting an interview with a single student unfeasible, but observing the language behaviors of students in small-group instructional settings would be more doable. The interactive techniques can be employed to see how successfully students employ language behaviors typical for each stage of language proficiency. These interactive techniques also work in conjunction with the strategies. For example, displaying pictures is helpful, but more learning occurs when students are actively manipulating the pictures by sequencing a storyboard.

◆ *Student Behaviors:* This is really the heart of the assessment. Given the challenge of consolidating language descriptors into a single page, I included only essential, key descriptors of a student's language usage at a given stage of development based upon the profiles drawn from ELD Content Standards. The individual descriptors of student behaviors have a two-fold benefit. They not only help identify a student's language level and stage of development but also equip the teacher with the necessary words to readily report and justify to colleagues the language level for a given student and the reasons to use specific accommodations.

◆ *Differentiated Strategies:* The strategies were drawn from a variety of sources with differentiating instruction for English language learners (Xu, 2010; Boyd-Batstone, 2006, 2009; Cummins, 2000, 2001; Fitzgerald & Noblit, 2000; and Krashen & Terrell, 1984). The intention is to provide teachers with instructional strategies appropriate to each level. Notice that the initial strategies are not relegated to the beginning and early intermediate stages. They continue to be useful at all levels but may be used with more complex vocabulary development, reading texts, and projects involving writing.

Who Will Use This Assessment Tool?

The Classroom Assessment of English Language Levels is for you if one of the following scenarios applies to you:

◆ Teachers with new students who are English language learners without assessment information
◆ Teachers who need a formative assessment tool that takes very little time to administer
◆ Teachers who want to pre-assess their students prior to administering a lengthy summative assessment
◆ Teachers who need appropriate strategies for differentiating instruction to accommodate the needs of English language learners in the classroom
◆ Teachers who wonder if their instruction helps their students' progress in their language proficiency
◆ Teachers looking to use small-group instruction as a vehicle for language assessment
◆ Elementary-school teachers needing interview questions to identify language levels of their students
◆ Secondary-level teachers who want to assess students without interrupting the flow of instruction
◆ School counselors needing to quickly identify approximate language levels of new arriving English language learners
◆ Administrators wanting a quick reference to see if their teachers are providing appropriate instruction for the English language learners in their classrooms

What Is in This Book?

Part 1 of this book (chapters 1–3) includes the introduction to the CALL with subsequent chapters providing detailed information about how to use the CALL, how to interpret the assessment information, and appropriate instruction that matches each stage of language proficiency.

Included in chapter 2 are the various components of the CALL in a more in-depth way. Here you will find the assessment tool and detailed descriptions of each of the parts and ways they contribute to assessment and instruction. Those components are the following:

♦ Levels and stages
♦ Duration
♦ Questions
♦ Interactive techniques
♦ Student behaviors
♦ Differentiated strategies

Chapter 3 provides step-by-step directions for how to use the CALL from two different perspectives. Ideally, a teacher will have the time to sit with a student for a couple of minutes to talk and assess the student's language level. This chapter demonstrates how to conduct an interview with a student and provides time-saving techniques for each level of the interview process. When teachers are too busy to conduct one-on-one direct interviews, there is another way. Teachers may use the tool for observing students in small-group instructional settings using a range of interactive techniques that match the students' language level. This may apply more to secondary-level teachers who work with much greater numbers of students. Included in this chapter is also the CALL Record Sheet as a supplemental tool for recording assessment data on a quarterly basis over the course of an academic year. Also be sure to look for time-saving tips and small-group instructional strategies that facilitate English language learners to demonstrate their language behaviors for assessment purposes.

Part 2 (chapters 4–8) devotes a whole chapter to each stage of language development from beginning to advanced proficiency. The characteristics of each stage are discussed as are the appropriate strategies and how to address each Common Core Listening and Speaking Standard in K–2, 3–5, 6–8, 9–10, and 11–12.

Chapter 4 and the following chapters provide an in-depth look at the language behaviors and appropriate teaching strategies for each level as aligned with the Common Core State Standards for Listening and Speaking, grades K–2, 3–5, 6–8, and 10–12. The beginning stage is characterized by a silent period in which the ELL is actively listening and acquiring basic oral language to communicate minimally. In this chapter, beginning stage language behaviors and instructional applications are provided. The instructional applications are as follows:

♦ Employing simple "caretaker" speech
♦ Using realia and visuals
♦ Showing meaning with gestures and Total Physical Response (TPR)
♦ Avoiding forcing speech
♦ Selecting books and reading with students

Each Common Core State Standard for Listening and Speaking grades K–12 is addressed for the beginning stage ELL.

Chapter 5 provides an in-depth discussion of the language behaviors at the early intermediate stage of language proficiency and the appropriate instructional applications in elementary-school, middle-school, and high-school settings. This stage is characterized by the ability to tell brief narratives. The English language learner operates predominantly in the oral language realm with some print language being used. Appropriate instructional applications for this level include the following:

♦ Using predictable books
♦ Selecting books with vivid illustrations
♦ Developing storyboard frames
♦ Employing interactive journals
♦ Creating chart stories
♦ Providing direct instruction of vocabulary

Each Common Core State Standard for Listening and Speaking grades K–12 is addressed for the early intermediate stage ELL.

Chapter 6 explores the language behaviors expected for the intermediate stage of language proficiency and the instructional applications that match. Speech at this stage is characterized by inserting details into oral language. Print literacy also becomes more prominently used to communicate messages. The appropriate instructional applications include the following:

♦ Tapping prior knowledge and experiences
♦ Developing initial study skills
♦ Using cognates
♦ Exploring word origins
♦ Writing for a purpose
♦ Using and creating media projects

Each Common Core State Standard for Listening and Speaking grades K–12 is addressed for the intermediate stage ELL.

Chapter 7 examines the shift from the intermediate to the early advanced stage of language proficiency and the appropriate instructional applications. The early advanced stage is often characterized by a high degree of language fluency within familiar subject areas or "comfort zones." When the topic changes to an unfamiliar subject, the language proficiency is more like intermediate stage behavior. This is a key and deceptive notion of assessment because a student can appear fully fluent to one teacher but not to another, depending on the degree of discipline-specific or academic language the student knows. The appropriate instructional applications at this stage include the following:

- Shifting focus from oral language to writing development
- Expanding study skills and individual learning strategies
- Conducting formal grammar instruction
- Implementing the full range of Specially Designed Academic Instruction in English (SDAIE) strategies

Each Common Core State Standard for Listening and Speaking grades K–12 is addressed for the early advanced stage ELL.

Chapter 8 caps the discussion of stages of language proficiency with the advanced stage. There are subtle differences between early advanced and advanced stages of language proficiency. A key difference is to what degree an ELL takes on a leadership role in a discussion. A leadership role may include posing questions to others and synthesizing the contributions of the group's participants. An advanced ELL demonstrates a high degree of comfort in social situations as characterized by being able to understand culturally embedded humor and to even tell jokes successfully. The appropriate instructional applications at this level include the following:

- Expanding academic vocabulary
- Refining writing skills
- Refining study and research skills
- Assigning more-complex projects

Each Common Core State Standard for Listening and Speaking grades K–12 is addressed for the advanced stage ELL.

The Classroom Assessment of Language Levels was developed for teachers as a ready to use, formative assessment tool of English language learners' language development. The focus is on what to teach a student at a given level. As Afflerbach & Clark (2011) stated so aptly, "Formative assessment, in the hands of talented teachers, provides information that can help shape diverse students' learning and achievement" (p. 307). This tool is not simply a way to identify language levels; it is designed to give direction to shape learning and achievement for English language learners.

2

The Components of the Classroom Assessment of Language Levels

The Classroom Assessment of Language Levels (Figure 2.1, pages 14–15) is a tool designed for speed and ease of use. From teachers' perspectives, rapid assessment is needed in order to begin appropriately differentiated instruction immediately. Teachers cannot wait weeks or months for large-scale assessment results to begin to address the strengths and needs of their students. From students' perspectives, whether they realize it or not, English language learners do not have time on their side either. They are arriving behind their grade level from the outset; therefore, the faster teachers can apply appropriate instruction based on assessment of language level, the quicker ELLs can get up to grade level competency.

Ease of use complements the need for quick assessment. A classroom teacher should be able to note student behaviors and appropriate strategies at a glance. The CALL is a single page for ready reference. More-comprehensive descriptors would mean lengthy pages of materials that may not be handy for a teacher to use. The teacher can keep a single sheet assessment at hand along with lesson notes or on a clipboard with roster sheets. Included with the CALL is a record sheet that allows the teacher the opportunity to record the progress of a student's language development in quarterly increments over the course of an academic year.

This is a teacher-friendly assessment tool. In just a few minutes of informal interaction with an ELL or observation of an ELL interacting in a small group, the teacher will be able to quickly identify the student's language level. There are no tests to administer, no special abbreviations to learn, and no elaborate

Figure 2.1 Classroom Assessment of Language Levels (CALL)

Level	Stage	Duration	Questions for Direct Interview	Interactive Techniques for Small-Group Observations
1	Beginning	6 months	• Yes/no questions: "Is this an apple?" • Fill in the blank (cloze): "This fruit is an _____."	• List items. • Categorize and sequence pictures.
2	Early Intermediate	3 months–1year	• Who, when, what, where questions: "Who is that?" "When did this happen?" • Open-ended questions: "What were you thinking?"	• Name attributes and essential features. • Retell events.
3	Intermediate	2–3 years	• Descriptive details • How, why questions: "How did she do that?" "Why did she do that?"	• Encourage inquiry. • Request explanations in writing.
4	Early Advanced	3–4 years	• Analysis and synthesis questions: "What is the difference . . . ? " "How are they the same . . . ? "What is the central theme here?"	• Solve problems.
5	Advanced	> 3 years	• All questions • Encourage student to pose questions	• Take leadership in collaborative groups. • Synthesize what others are saying.

Student Behaviors	Differentiated Strategies
• Can be silent • Offers yes/no responses • Can name objects • Offers 1 to 2 word responses • Shows comprehension by following directions	• Use simple speech, caretaker speech. (p. 50) • Use realia, visuals, meaningful gestures (TPR). (p. 51) • Do not force speech. (p. 52) • Read to student. (p. 52)
• Speaks in simple sentences • Retells story events • Reads basic vocabulary and simple sentences • Make frequent grammatical errors in speech	• Use all of the above. (p. 66) • Use predictable books. (p. 67) • Use books with vivid illustrations. (p. 67) • Develop storyboard frames. (p. 68) • Use interactive journals. (p. 68) • Create chart stories. (p. 69) • Provide direct vocabulary (p. 71) instruction.
• Retells using expanded vocabulary • Explains main ideas and details • Summarizes texts • Makes comparisons • Defines new vocabulary	• Use all of the above. (p. 95) • Tap experiences. (p. 95) • Teach study skills. (p. 96) • Use cognates. (p. 98) • Explore word origins. (p. 98) • Teach writing for a purpose. (p. 99) • Use/create media. (p. 101)
• Appears to be orally fluent • Uses limited academic vocabulary and language • Needs to attain grade level reading/writing in academic areas • Analyzes, compares, contrasts	• Shift focus from oral to written language development. (p. 124) • Expand study/learning skills. (p. 125) • Provide formal grammar instruction. (p. 125) • Use SDAIE strategies. (p. 126)
• Comprehends content material • Generates discussions • Is socially comfortable • Reads and writes at grade level	• Expand academic vocabulary. (p. 148) • Refine writing skills. (p. 148) • Refine research/study skills. (p. 148) • Complete complex projects. (p. 149)

recording procedures. On the same page are the suggested instructional strategies that align with the student's language level.

In developing the CALL instrument, considering economy of size meant deciding not only what to include but also what *not* to include. For example, this tool does not address spelling with any detail. It will refer to characteristic spelling for a given language level but was not designed to assess spelling. Facets of language development such as spelling call for more involved assessment protocols. Accurate spelling assessment is an important way to identify instructional strategies for encoding language. Gentry (1996) and Bear, Invernezzi, and Templeton (2000) have already addressed spelling assessment. Nevertheless, the CALL is for initial rapid assessment.

Components of the CALL

The purpose of this chapter is to define terms and to provide an overview of each component of the CALL. The single page of CALL is organized into a six-column table that includes the following headings:

◆ Level
◆ Stages
◆ Duration
◆ Questioning/Interactive Techniques
◆ Student Behaviors
◆ Differentiated Strategies

Note that the CALL is also available as a Free Download on Eye On Education's website (see page xi).

Level
Language levels are numbered 1 to 5 with 5 being the highest or nearest to fully fluent level. There are several reasons for including numbered levels in the assessment, including generating ready reference, communication with others, and quantifiable data.

Many sets of terms are used to classify language proficiency (CELDT 1999; WIDA, 2012), but using numbered levels is universal and gives the assessor a ready "handle" on language level. Some terms related to language level from the assessments cited above are as follows: *entering, emerging, developing, expanding,* or *building.* The terms by themselves don't actually convey the scale they refer to. It is far easier for a teacher to think of a number than a specific term related to language level. A number, in contrast, is much less ambiguous, especially once the scale and range are established, as with levels 1 through 5, with 1 as the lowest and 5 as the highest.

The use of numbered levels also facilitates communicating with colleagues and the student's family members. There is no need to translate program-specific terms when referencing a number. With all of the various assessment programs in the field, even the initiated, such as other teachers, administrators, counselors,

Figure 2.2 First and Second Semester Comparison of ELL Score Levels

Semester (N=20)	Level 1	Level 2	Level 3	Level 4	Level 5
1st Semester	3 (15%)	7 (35%)	8 (40%)	2 (10%)	0 (0%)
2nd Semester	1 (5%)	5 (20%)	9 (45%)	3 (15%)	2 (10%)

and school psychologists, might need some orientation to specific terminology of a given assessment tool. Referencing a numbered level can quickly inform colleagues about your students.

Consider communicating with a family member of an ELL. Most likely, the family member is an English language learner too. Attempting to translate an ambiguous term such as *building* might prove confusing. It may not carry the same connotation across languages. Think of the literal image that *building* creates in the mind. Imagine saying to a parent, "Your child is at the *building* level of language proficiency." Now try to clarify that literal image in order to explain a language level. It is just not that easily done. Although it sounds fine in our educational lexicon, it does not easily connect with language development for the uninitiated parent of an ELL. Using a numbered scale is a much clearer reference point. For example, "Your child is at level 3 on a five-point scale of language levels."

Finally, the universal nature of numbers provides a means to record quantitative (numerical) data. This can help with teacher-research projects such as analyzing simple descriptive statistics about a program. An example of using simple descriptive statistics would be to compare average scores across programs to show simple statistical comparisons, such as effect sizes, for a particular intervention. Another example would be to show different percentages of scores across language groups for comparison purposes. Note in Figure 2.2 (above) how a teacher can record the language proficiency growth of ELLs from semester to semester using numeric levels.

Stages

The CALL has five stages that correspond to the numbered levels: (1) beginning, (2) early intermediate, (3) intermediate, (4) early advanced, (5) advanced. They give a name to each level and help provide more detail in identifying where an ELL is along the continuum from beginning to advanced.

One might ask "Why stages?" and "Why five stages?" The concept of stages comes from the field of cognitive psychology and is applied to the notion of developmentally appropriate practice. *Stage* is a useful term but it does have limitations. Purcell-Gates (2004) discussed the limitations of age-level stages with regard to language development. She argued that age-related lockstep stages are an abstraction of the reality of language development. Language actually develops more in phases than in stages. Phases overlap and even reoccur in new situations. For example, an ELL may show a high level of fluency in a particular field, such as sports, but when the ELL is introduced to a new field, such as geography, the words are not there and the student begins to exhibit behaviors from an earlier stage. Understanding the limitations of the term *stages*, I still chose to retain it because the term was applied to the use of ELD Content Standards.

In accordance with the NCLB (2001), assessment of English language learners is mandated. Murphy, Bailey, and Butler (2006) evaluated English learner assessment in response to NCLB, and they established a link between ELD content standards and applied linguistics. They employed the use of five stages of language development that laid the groundwork for ELD content standards.

Are five stages necessary? The answer is yes and no. Experience has taught me that it is difficult to juggle five different categories for instruction. Teachers tend to differentiate their instruction into three categories, roughly beginning, intermediate, and advanced. Teachers can easily group students for instruction around beginning, intermediate, and advanced instruction. However, that doesn't address this question: "Why have the two additional stages, early intermediate and early advanced?" Grouping students for instruction is one aspect of assessment. Identifying language level to determine specific instruction is another aspect of assessment that requires more precision. Identification of early intermediate and early advanced students provides a more nuanced identification of instructional needs.

Certain aspects of language require more nuanced information. Reading and writing, for instance, are very broad, deep aspects of language development. Being able to identify an ELL as early intermediate or early advanced allows the teacher to make more informed choices about when to introduce specific subjects, such as greater use of adjectives and adverbs. The five stages of language development are defined in the student behaviors section.

Duration

Duration refers to the expected amount of time an ELL will remain at a particular stage under normal circumstances. This kind of information adds to the assessment in several ways. Periodically, a teacher can review a student's language level to determine how the student is progressing toward advanced proficiency. If the teacher suspects that the student is lingering too long at a particular stage, the teacher can employ a specific intervention. Conversely, knowing the duration can help document whether a student is making rapid progress, or faster than expected progress, toward advanced proficiency.

The research of Collier and Thomas (1987) was used in this assessment of duration. I aligned the levels and stages with the duration, in months to years, one could reasonably expect a student to remain at a level, assuming that no other factors impeded language development.

Questions

Questions are invitations for interaction; however, certain types of questions are more appropriate for students at earlier stages. For example, a teacher who asked a student at the beginning level of proficiency to explain his or her thinking on an issue would predictably get a confused stare and an awkward pause as a response. Because the beginner by definition can respond with only gestures, a yes or a no, or a one-word answer, the teacher needs to ask a question that calls for that type of response. The differentiated questioning initiates a conversation for assessment; the questions are also used in conjunction with strategies at a glance, discussed below.

Using differentiated questions during an assessment facilitates the process by giving the student a way to respond according to a particular stage of language development. Questions need to be tailored to the student's stage of language development for very practical reasons. Students at the beginning stage of language development can respond with only a limited set of words and gestures. And students at the early intermediate stage will provide only short answers or brief narratives in response to questions. Consequently, asking students at the beginning stage to retell a narrative or describe their thoughts at length would most likely result in blank stares. So questions must be differentiated as follows:

Beginning Stage
◆ *Questions:* Yes or no (*Is this an apple?*); either/or (*Is this an apple or is it a peach?*)

Early Intermediate Stage
◆ *Wh-Questions:* Who? (*Who ate the apple? Who gave the apple away?*), When? (*When did she eat the apple? When did he give her the apple?*), What? (*What happened? What did she eat? What did he give her?*), Where? (*Where did she eat the apple? Where was she?*)
◆ *Open-Ended Questions: What were you thinking as I read the story? What did you picture in your mind? What do you think will happen next? What would you do?*

Intermediate Stage
◆ *Questions:* How? (*How did she get there? How would you solve the problem?*); Why? (*Why do you think so? Why did she travel so far out of her way?*)

Early Advanced Stage
◆ *Questions:* Summary (*What happened here? Tell me your solution.*); Analysis (*What were the steps of that solution?*); Evaluation (*Is this the best solution? Justify your thinking.*)

Advanced Stage
◆ *Questions:* Posing questions to others (*What questions do you have for the group?*); Synthesis (*What do you hear the group saying about this issue? Based on your reading, what are the important ideas being addressed?*)

Interactive Techniques

Busy teachers do not always have the luxury of sitting down with their students one-on-one to ask questions. This is particularly the case with teachers at the middle- and high-school levels. It is not uncommon for a teacher to work with more than 200 students during a school day. However, the teacher can observe and assess students' language behaviors using a range of interactive techniques in small-group instructional settings. The following interactive techniques are leveled according to language stages. The techniques include a range of activities, such as listing and categorizing items at the beginning level, employing problem-solving approaches at intermediate, and even leading small-group discussions at advanced stages of language proficiency.

As students work in small-group instructional settings, the teacher can observe to what extent the English language learners successfully interact with their peers. The following are selected techniques according to stages of language proficiency:

Beginning Stage
♦ *Interactive Techniques:* Completing fill-in-the-blank sentences, listing or naming items, categorizing, sequencing story cards

Early Intermediate Stage
♦ *Interactive Techniques:* Describing, retelling, responding to reading, making predictions

Intermediate Stage
♦ *Interactive Techniques:* Asking questions, supplying descriptive details, paraphrasing orally and in writing

Early Advanced Stage
♦ *Interactive Techniques:* Summarizing, analyzing, evaluating, problem-posing approaches

Advanced Stage
♦ *Interactive techniques:* Posing questions to others, taking leadership in group discussions, synthesizing

Questioning strategies and interactive techniques are frequently used together for instruction. Both questions and interactive techniques can be effectively modified to accommodate the language level of English language learners. For example, a key questioning strategy for ELLs at beginning and early intermediate stages would be to ask what is the name of an object, allowing them to provide one-word answers. In addition, some related interactive techniques would be listing items, sequencing, and categorizing pictures. These interactive strategies also work in conjunction with the differentiated instructional strategies. For example, displaying pictures is helpful, but more learning occurs when students are actively manipulating the pictures by sequencing a storyboard.

At more advanced stages, the questions and interactive techniques are differentiated to move the students from simply responding to short-answer questions to providing more expanded explanations with details. Further, they are expected to increase their repertoire of language use to reflect on their words and the words of others. They are asked to summarize, analyze, and evaluate. Finally, advanced stage students are encouraged to take leadership roles in discussions, to pose questions to the group, and to synthesize what is being expressed.

The selected types of questions and interactive techniques in the CALL function as invitations to ELLs to share what they know and can do. Additionally, they are like differentiated prompts that give a teacher readily usable information about a student's expected language-usage behavior. It is important to reiterate that these are not lockstep techniques that are apparent only at a designated stage. An ELL may respond in a variety of ways. The differentiation is based on normal expected abilities and behaviors at a given stage. For example, a beginning stage student may evaluate what is being said but probably would not have the vocabulary to express the evaluation fluently. An accurate assessment would be based on a student's demonstration that he or she can respond to the suggested types of questions and express her or his thinking fluently in English using those techniques at that particular level.

Student Behaviors

This is really the heart of the assessment. Given the challenge of consolidating language descriptors into a single page, the assessment included only essential, key descriptors of a student's language usage at a given stage of development. The individual descriptors of student behaviors have a two-fold benefit. They not only help identify a student's language level and stage of development but also equip a teacher with terminology to readily report observations that contribute to justifying the assessment to colleagues.

The following is a summary of expected student behaviors at each stage of language development:

Beginning stage students are characterized by silence and single-word responses. They will answer yes or no questions and follow directions when they understand a command or directive. Meaningful gestures used by both the teacher and the student for communication are extremely helpful at this stage. Very little written communication takes place at this level. Language development is primarily oral.

Early intermediate stage students are characterized by being able to communicate with sentences marked by frequent grammatical errors. The ability to formulate a short narrative indicates the early intermediate stage. I was always able to tell that students had reached this stage when they became tattletales. They could tell me what had happened on the playground or explain why they were unhappy about something or someone. Students at this stage begin to read and write using phonology for spelling and syntactical patterns based on their first language.

Intermediate stage students are characterized by expressing lengthier narratives that employ more detail. They use complete sentences that might include an array of adjectives. They spell more conventionally and use syntax with more conventional word order. Students at this level can read lengthier passages for understanding and write multiple paragraphs but need direct help with vocabulary and grammar.

Early advanced stage students appear to be operating at grade level. They may be highly fluent in certain subject areas, but when they are introduced to a new subject area, they may struggle and need specific vocabulary help. Students at this level benefit from learning to use resource material, search engines, and reference materials. They need to develop a deeper understanding of vocabulary in content areas on their own. They can be more self-directed learners at this stage.

Advanced stage students operate at or above grade level. They are more competent in social situations characterized by telling and understanding jokes that play on words. They can be pushed to synthesize what a group is discussing. They still need vocabulary development with unfamiliar subjects and will occasionally draw a blank on how to express themselves.

Differentiated Strategies

The CALL provides teachers with instructional strategies appropriate to each level of language proficiency. This book also presents more in depth instructional recommendations that are aligned with Common Core State Standards as well as leveled according to language proficiency

To clarify terminology in this book, I use the terms *strategies* and *activities*. The term *strategies* can be ambiguous because it applies to both teachers and students. Teachers use teaching strategies, and students use learning strategies. However, in this book, I use the term *strategies* primarily to designate "what teachers do." And I use the term *activities* to designate "what students do" in response to teacher strategies. I make this distinction because this pertains to an assessment tool designed to inform instruction. The strategies listed below tend to be from the teacher's perspective as they align with the appropriate stage of language development. In the second section of this book, I go into detail about how to apply these strategies to a selected section of the Common Core State Standards, K–12. I chose the listening and speaking standards because that is where instruction begins with English language learners.

The differentiated strategies are cumulative by design. This means that a recommended strategy for beginning and early intermediate stages can also be appropriate for more advanced stages. For example, the use of vivid illustrations is essential for students at beginning and early intermediate stages; but they are most helpful at intermediate and advanced stages as well. Conversely, the strategies unique to more advanced stages, such as asking ELLs to synthesize what a group of students had just been discussing, are not appropriate at earlier stages. You would ask an advanced ELL to synthesize a group discussion, but with a beginning ELL, you could just get a blank stare.

Another feature to note is that the differentiated strategies section works in conjunction with the questioning/interactive techniques section. An example of a strategy using visuals at the beginning stage would be to categorize pictures or sequence story pictures as suggested in the questioning/interactive techniques section.

The following are differentiated strategies at a glance for immediate instruction. These are essential strategies, so the list is not intended to be comprehensive. Throughout this book, I will provide a detailed explanation and steps for implementation for each of the suggested strategies.

Beginning Stage
♦ Use simple speech, caretaker speech. Use short sentences accompanied by meaningful gestures.
♦ Use realia (real objects in order to tap all senses), visuals (pictures, diagrams, models, media), and meaningful gestures (total physical response [Asher, 1969]).
♦ Do not force a student to speak English. Demanding that a student "speak English" frightens and discourages a child who would like nothing more than to be able to communicate freely.
♦ Read to the student. Use picture books that have engaging stories.

Early Intermediate Stage
♦ Continue to use all of the above.
♦ Use predictable books. Books with speech patterns, repetition, and predictability provide language that students can use and read more easily.
♦ Use books with vivid illustrations. The quality of the pictures enhances students' ability to understand what is going on in the story. With informational texts, vivid illustrations are vital to making the content understandable.
♦ Use graphic organizers. Develop storyboard frames, tree maps, and cluster maps to diagram the relationships among various elements of a text.
♦ Write with interactive journals. This is not designed for full process writing; it is meant to be a personal, informal dialogue. The purpose is to create a shared writing experience in which a teacher's written responses provide an active model of how to express one's thoughts in writing.
♦ Create chart stories. When class members compose a story collaboratively on a large sheet of paper, the teacher often records the words of the students.
♦ Provide direct vocabulary instruction. Explicitly teach key vocabulary before a lesson, and follow up with a fluency activity and review.

Intermediate Stage
- Continue to use all of the above.
- Tap prior experience. Press for details about what the students know before beginning instruction on a topic.
- Teach study skills. Show students how to take notes, use reference materials, and mark up reading material.
- Use cognates. Learn and use the words that carry across the students' home languages to English. It increases comprehension.
- Explore word origins. Studying word etymologies tells the story behind words and helps students identify root meanings.
- Encourage writing for a purpose. Invite students to write about real-life topics that relate to their cultural settings.
- Use and create media. Information technology is global. Have students become authors of their world using up-to-date media tools.

Early Advanced Stage
- Shift literacy development focus from oral to written language development. Provide as many opportunities for writing as possible. For example, while teaching a lesson, ask students to paraphrase the learning in writing, rather than orally.
- Expand study and learning skills instruction. Teach the skills needed for using double-entry journals, establishing personal instructional goals, and using advanced search tools. Teach students how to learn vocabulary independently.
- Provide formal grammar instruction. Teach noun-verb agreement, syntax, and compound and complex sentence structure.
- Employ SDAIE strategies. Specially Designed Academic Instruction in English was conceived to address content area instruction and literacy development at a high level of academic achievement. SDAIE is a collection of strategies including preview/review, primary language support, use of realia and visuals, explicit vocabulary instruction, collaborative projects, and formative/summative assessment.

Advanced Stage
- Expand academic vocabulary. Introduce vocabulary with each new subject area.
- Refine writing skills. Provide multiple forms for writing independently, including narrative, informational, poetry, and song.
- Refine research and study skills. Introduce and use a wide range of databases specific to the subject area. Teach how to write research reports.
- Assign complex projects. Put students in leadership roles with projects such as creating a multi-authored newsletter, working on collaborative science projects, or using problem-solving approaches to mathematics.

All of those components have been condensed into a single table for quick assessment and ease of use.

3

Ways to Conduct an Assessment: Direct Interview and Indirect Small-Group Observation

The Classroom Assessment of Language Levels is designed to provide busy teachers with in-the-moment information about a student's English language level and appropriate differentiated instruction. Teachers may conduct brief one-to-one interviews or use the tool to observe students in small-group settings. This formative assessment utilizes leveled questions and interactive techniques to gather observations of student language behaviors. Assessment with this tool involves comparing observations of student language behaviors at various levels and aligning key behaviors to instructional strategies. Accompanying the CALL is a record sheet divided into quarters of the academic year to track language development of each English learner in the classroom.

Unfortunately, instruction and assessment are often perceived as competing for the same time, rather than being complementary, in classroom settings. Time is a fundamental challenge to the classroom teacher. Teachers struggle to optimize the time they are allotted. Ideally, assessment should be unobtrusive and a regular part of the instructional sequence. Skilled teachers are continually looking for ways to maximize instructional time while gathering assessment data to make informed decisions. The challenge, therefore, is to conduct quality assessment that does not hinder or impede instruction.

This chapter will demonstrate how to use the CALL in ways that complement instruction and provide the assessment information needed to differentiate according to students' needs. It will also explain how to use the accompanying record sheet for quarterly progress updates.

Figure 3.1 Questioning and Interactive Techniques

Level and Stages	Questions for Interview	Interactive Techniques for Small Groups
Level 1: Beginning	Yes or no questions: *Do you like this picture? Do you play soccer?* Either/or questions: *Is this a girl or a boy? Is she kicking a ball or walking?* Fill in the blank (cloze): *The girl is kicking a _____ . (soccer ball, football, ball)*	Give directions. *Point to the girl. Point to the trees in the background.* List items. *What is this? And what is this? (Point to different items; repeat.)* *What items can you name?* Categorize or sequence objects or pictures. *Put these items in the same groups. You decide how to group them. Tell me about your grouping.*
Level 2: Early Intermediate	Who, when, what, where, questions: *Who do you think is in the picture? Tell me about her.* *When do you think she played with the ball? What time of day?* *What is happening in the picture?* *Where do you think this happened?* Open-ended questions: *What were you thinking about?* *What do you think is happening?*	Identify essential features. *Tell me what you see in this picture.* Retell events.

How to Use the Classroom Assessment of Language Levels

This tool can be used in several ways, depending on the instructional setting and the needs of the instructor. Flexibility is an advantage of this assessment tool. For example, a teacher may use the CALL in a one-on-one interview. It can also be used to observe one or more students indirectly as they demonstrate their language ability in a small-group setting.

Sitting down to talk with an individual student affords the opportunity to get significant instructional information. In just a few moments, it is possible to identify the language level of a child and to match instruction to the student's strengths and needs. This can readily be done fairly easily in elementary-school settings because of group rotations and moments during the instructional day

Figure 3.1 Questioning and Interactive Techniques *(continued)*

Level 3: Intermediate	How, why questions: *How would you change this picture? Tell me about it. How do you think she did that? Why did you say that?*	Encourage inquiry. *Where do you think this picture came from? What do you think this picture is about?* Expand descriptive details. *Tell me more about that. Add some details. Can you say that in a different way?* Request explanations in writing. *Can you write what you see? Please share it with me.*
Level 4: Early Advanced	Analysis and synthesis questions: *What is going on in this picture? What is special about this picture? What are some unique elements of this picture? Is this picture like any others you've seen? Tell me about it.*	Solve problems. *What would you do to take a picture like this one? How would you retake this picture? Picture yourself in the picture. What would you be doing? How would you look?*
Level 5: Advanced	All questions: Students should be able to respond fluently and appropriately to all the above questions. Students' questions: *What questions do you have about this picture? What else can you tell me about this picture?*	Take leadership in collaborative groups. *Please guide the discussion about the picture.* Synthesize what others have said. *In your own words, describe what the group discussed. Can you sum up what each person said? (May be done orally or in writing.)*

when students work individually. However, in secondary-school settings, one-on-one interviews are very difficult to arrange because of a number of factors. Some negative factors may include large class sizes, short instructional time slots with passing periods, or possibly shyness on the part of a student in front of a teacher. On the positive side, factors may include extensive use of collaborative small groups for instruction, or classroom approaches comprised predominantly of direct, explicit instruction. Given such factors, indirect observation of a child in a small-group setting might be a preferable way to use the CALL. Sample questions and interactive techniques matched to language levels are shown in Figure 3.1 (pages 26–27).

How to Conduct an Assessment

The next section provides detailed directions for conducting a direct one-on-one interview and an indirect observation of one or more students in a small-group setting. Following the how-to section, I discuss interpreting student behaviors, assessing language levels, and recording assessment data on a quarterly basis. Let's take a closer look at each way to use the CALL.

Direct One-on-One Interview

This technique involves sitting down with a student, away from the hustle and bustle of classroom activity, to talk and listen. The teacher asks questions, can use interactive techniques, and listens for key indicators of language behaviors.

Materials Needed
◆ Classroom Assessment of Language Levels tool
◆ A vivid picture or illustration to initiate discussion
◆ A notepad and pen to record the assessment

Procedures
1. Keep the CALL handy for ready reference for questioning techniques, student behaviors, and aligned strategies for instruction.

Figure 3.2 Sample Photograph to Initiate Discussion

Source: Photo courtesy of Kathryn Boyd-Batstone. Used with permission. www.kathrynboydbatstone.com

2. Select a vivid picture or illustration to give context to the conversation. (I like to use photos because they provide a rich array of descriptive material to talk about. However, a vivid illustration from a picture book will serve the same purpose.)
3. Show the picture to the student.
4. Begin with a question or an interactive technique from the beginning level of the CALL. If the student responds readily, move on to the next level.
5. If the student struggles to respond to a question, stop and record the level of proficiency. You may ask another question of similar type to be sure that you were understood, but if the student can no longer respond, the questioning should stop at this point.
6. Note the language behaviors the student exhibited by writing down one or more of the descriptive phrases at that level. (In the event of a borderline case, go with the lower level because it would just mean reinforcement of specific strategies the student could benefit from.)
7. Select the appropriate strategies for instruction at the student's assessed level.

To give context to questions and interactive techniques for the above procedure, I recommend using a picture. The specific picture is the teacher's choice. I like the picture in Figure 3.2 because it provides lots of possibilities for questions and interaction.

Figure 3.3 (below) shows sample beginning-level questions based on the photograph of the girl kicking the soccer ball.

Figure 3.3 Level 1: Beginning Questions and Student Behaviors

Questions	Student Behaviors
Yes or no questions:	Can be silent
Do you like this picture? Do you play soccer?	Offers yes or no responses
	Can name objects
Either/or questions:	Offers one- to two-word responses
Is this a girl or a boy? Is she kicking a ball or walking?	Shows comprehension by following directions
Fill in the blank (cloze):	
The girl is kicking a _____ . *(soccer ball, football, ball)*	

At the beginning level, students tend to be silent and use a very limited range of words. Often with beginning ELLs, responses are limited to gestures or a nod of the head representing yes or no. Sometimes there is no response, only a silent stare. This is why questions must be limited to yes or no. Students at this level will recognize a possible response that is embedded in an either/or question. When an ELL hears, "Is she kicking the ball or walking?" the student needs only to select and repeat the answer he or she thinks is correct. Either/or questions help with those words that are on the "tip of the tongue" but require a little help. Cloze, or fill in the blank, type questions expect that the ELL knows the word and thus provide full sentences minus key words.

Beginning interactive techniques parallel the questions. Showing with gestures comes before telling with words. For example, if an ELL is silent, giving directions invites gestures that show understanding and specific language behaviors such as pointing to identify a picture. This is a non-verbal language behavior that indicates understanding, or a lack of understanding, depending on where the student points. If the student can respond with yes or no, he or she may include a pointing gesture as reinforcement. If the student can name items in a picture, an appropriate interactive technique is to list as many items as possible. Listing items, which is an appropriate language behavior for this level, allows the ELL to name things without worrying about making up complete sentences. Further, categorizing pictures or objects allows the ELL to show a deeper level of understanding. The student is not just naming items but also showing their relationships and, if possible, coming up with a new word to label each category. Level 1 does not require full sentence explanations, just labeling with single words or phrases.

Now let's look at questions and behaviors for level 2 (Figure 3.4).

Time-Saving Strategy: Mark Up a Copy of the Quick Assessment for Each ELL

Keep multiple copies of the CALL on hand, one for each student. Write the student's name and date at the top. When assessing a student, mark up the page with checks for the types of questions or interactive techniques you used. Circle the language behaviors that you observed. Keep notes on the page. Later, use the CALL Record Sheet to record the date of the assessment, the language level and stage, a language behavior that supported the assessment, and a recommended instructional strategy.

Figure 3.4 Level 2: Early Intermediate Questions and Student Behaviors

Questions	Student Behaviors
Who, when, what, where questions: *Who do you think is in the picture? Tell me about her. When do you think she played with the ball? What time of day?* *What is happening in the picture?* *Where do you think this happened?* Open-ended questions: *What were you thinking about?* *What do you think is happening?*	Speaks in simple sentences Retells story events Reads basic vocabulary, simple sentences Makes frequent grammatical errors in speech

Early Intermediate ELLs begin to put together words and phrases into simple sentences. The moment students could complain about an infraction on the playground, or a disagreement with another student, I knew that they were at this level. The transition from beginning to early intermediate can happen relatively quickly; therefore, examples of this behavior can appear at moments such as after recess breaks or between instructional times.

The language behaviors that an ELL exhibits at this point should be characterized by simple sentences with frequent grammatical errors. When assessing, using wh- questions that ask "who," "when," "what," and "where" invite full-sentence responses. They encourage students to form brief narratives or explanations of what they want to say.

The value of using open-ended questions at this stage is that they allow students to express themselves. There is no need to look for a predetermined answer. I recall once using another assessment tool that showed a woman holding a baby. As evaluator, I was scripted to ask, "Who is in the picture?" The predetermined answer was "a mother." But the student said, "She's a female." I was required to mark the answer as wrong; however, the language behavior the student exhibited was clearly beyond the level of the question and answer the assessment tool posed. If I had been permitted to use an open-ended question, such as "What can you tell me about this picture?," I would have gained more information about the student's language level. When using open-ended questions, a teacher is less concerned with specific content than with the extent to which students can use sentences to express themselves. The interactive technique is very similar. It simply directs a student to talk about a picture, thus opening up space to say as much as possible.

Let's move on to level 3 questions and behaviors (Figure 3.5, below).

Time-Saving Strategy: Begin with an Open-Ended Question
Rather than begin the assessment at level 1 and march through the tool sequentially; begin with an open-ended question, such as "What can you tell me about this picture?" If the student silently stares at the picture, then go back to the questions and interactive techniques for a beginning level ELL. If the student replies with simple sentences and frequent grammatical errors, you can expect that he or she is at level 2, early intermediate. However, if the student uses complete sentences with few errors and details, you can safely assume that the student is at a higher language level.

Figure 3.5 Level 3: Intermediate Questions and Student Behaviors

Questions	Student Behaviors
How, why questions:	Retells using expanded vocabulary
How would you change this picture? Tell me about it.	Identifies main ideas and details
	Can summarize
How do you think she did that?	Makes comparisons
Why did you say that?	Defines new vocabulary

There are several key differences between early intermediate and intermediate levels of fluency. Those differences include the use of descriptive details and the frequency of errors in oral and written communication. An ELL at the early intermediate level will speak in simple sentences and write using repetitive, high-frequency phrases such as "I like dogs. I like cats. I like . . . (fill in the blank)." In contrast, an ELL at the intermediate level of fluency would employ more descriptive details, use some adjectives, and show greater variety in sentence structure.

Interestingly, spelling might be deceptive. A student who does not take risks with spelling may appear to be orally fluent but write using only simple, repetitive sentences. A student who might appear to be shy or reserved orally might write extensively with little regard for conventions.

Use how and why questions so ELLs can demonstrate their ability to provide more descriptive details.

Figure 3.6 (below) shows questions and behaviors for Level 4.

Figure 3.6 Level 4: Early Advanced Questions and Student Behaviors

Questions	Student Behaviors
Analysis and synthesis questions: *What is going on in this picture? What is special about this picture?* *What are some unique elements of this picture?* *Is this picture like any others you've seen? Tell me about it.*	Appears to be orally fluent Uses limited academic vocabulary and language Needs to attain grade level reading and writing in academic areas

Students at the early advanced stage appear to be quite orally fluent. They are particularly fluent in their comfort zones—areas in which they have a high degree of knowledge and experience. However, the moment they step out of their comfort zones and grapple with unfamiliar subjects, they no longer display the same level of fluency.

This is a very common occurrence that all people experience. Think of the last time you went to your car mechanic and tried to explain what was wrong with your vehicle. You may have substituted automotive terms, such as *distributor* or *carburetor*, with words such as *thingamabob* or *doohickey*. You may have described the sounds with grunts and whistles because you did not have the vocabulary to properly convey what was going wrong with the car engine.

During assessments, teachers want to figuratively move ELLs outside their linguistic comfort zones to see what they need to learn. This is not mean-spirited or "gotcha" type assessment. It is exploring the boundaries of the student's language abilities. By asking higher-order questions, such as those designed to elicit analysis, comparisons, and synthesis, teachers move discussion beyond descriptive vocabulary. By asking what is going on and how does this work, teachers encourage language behaviors that exhibit more complex uses of thought and language. When teachers ask students to compare what they see to something else, the context expands to what students imagine beyond the page.

If a student begins to stammer and struggle, then the student is at the early advanced stage. If the student responds fluently with few pauses, then continue to the next level.

Figure 3.7 shows the questions and behaviors for level 5, advanced.

Time-Saving Strategy: Ask One Question with Follow-Up Prompts
Although a variety of questions could be asked at this point, a single question can get students to say all that is necessary to demonstrate their level of proficiency. An efficient use of time at this level is to concentrate on a single question, such as "What is going on here?" and then use follow-up prompts, such as "Tell me more," "Why did you say that?," "What did you mean by . . . ? " The key is to get students talking at their highest level. It is not about asking every suggested question because it is listed on the assessment tool.

Figure 3.7 Level 5: Advanced Questions and Student Behaviors

Questions	Student Behaviors
All questions: (The student should be able to respond fluently and appropriately to all previous levels of questions.) Students' questions: *What questions do you have about this picture?* *What else can you tell me about this picture?*	Comprehends content material Generates discussions Is socially comfortable Reads and writes at grade level

Students at the advanced stage have demonstrated proficiency in many ways. They respond appropriately to a range of questions. They are fluent in their responses. They show the ability to convey their thoughts and ideas fluently. A teacher may find that talking with a student at this stage is like having a free and easy conversation because the student is comfortable in social situations.

The assessment takes a turn at this point to having the student initiate questions. With previous levels, the teacher initiated the questions and noted the responses. At this point, the teacher invites the formulation of questions in order to hand the lead over to the student.

Something to look for at this level is humor. Expressing and understanding humor is a culturally embedded, complex language behavior. If you note that a student points out something funny about the picture, ask him or her to tell you about what is so funny. If the student can formulate a joke or a play on words, she or he is highly advanced.

Time-Saving Strategy: Share a Joke

As stated above, humor is a complex language behavior that is culturally embedded and sometimes dictated by current events. Think of how situational political humor is. Have a joke at the ready to share with the student to see if he or she gets the punch line. AhaJokes.com (www.ahajokes.com) offers clean jokes across a wide range of topics. Just be aware that students may laugh even if they don't get a joke because they don't want to offend in a social setting. Ask them if they know any jokes in English that they could share.

Indirect Observation of Students in Small Groups

As stated previously, in many classroom settings it is not feasible to conduct a direct one-on-one interview. This is especially the case in secondary classrooms with large class sizes and brief passing periods. A classroom teacher needs to be able to manage instruction and indirectly observe student language behaviors at the same time.

Certainly teachers are always observing student behaviors, but even quick assessment of students is virtually impossible to do effectively while conducting whole-class instruction. Therefore, I recommend conducting indirect observation of students in small-group learning situations. Whole-group instruction is often followed by small-group discussions or project development. This is an ideal time to watch how students are using language and to conduct a Classroom Assessment of Language Levels.

The following technique provides ways to maintain small-group instruction while assessing the language level of one or more English language learners.

Materials Needed
♦ Classroom Assessment of Language Levels tool
♦ Small-group discussion topic or collaborative project
♦ A notepad and pen to record the assessment

Procedures
1. Keep the CALL handy for ready reference for questioning techniques, student behaviors, and aligned strategies for instruction.
2. Organize students into small groups (four to six in a group). Consider whether you want the students who are the focus of your observation to be in the same small group or in different groups. If you choose different groups, try to place them near each other so that you need only swivel to observe and listen to language behaviors.
3. Give the students a discussion topic related to your regular instructional content. Other options might include assigning a collaborative project or problem-solving activity that requires a high degree of student-to-student interaction.

4. Begin by observing the focus students' initial use of language in the small group(s). Write down the student language behaviors that you observe.
5. If the focus students remain silent while other students are interacting, insert yourself into the small-group discussion by posing a question. Begin with a level 1 beginning interactive technique, such as listing items.
6. If the student readily responds, move on to the next level.
7. If the student struggles to respond to a question, stop and record the level of proficiency. You may ask another question of a similar type to be sure that you were understood, but if the student can no longer respond, the questioning should stop at this point.
8. Continue to note the language behaviors the student exhibited by writing down one or more of the descriptive phrases at that level. (In the event of a borderline case, assess the ELL at the lower level because it would call for reinforcement of specific strategies the student could benefit from.)
9. Select the appropriate strategies for instruction at the student's assessed level.
10. Use the CALL Record Sheet to record the date of the assessment and the language level number and stage, note a specific language behavior that indicated the language level, and note a selected appropriate strategy for instruction.

Figures 3.8 through 3.12 show sample techniques based again on the photograph of the girl with the soccer ball (page 28). Let's first look at some beginning-level techniques (Figure 3.8, below).

Figure 3.8 Level 1: Beginning Techniques and Behaviors

Interactive Techniques	Student Behaviors
Give directions	Can be silent
Point to the girl. Point to the trees in the background.	Offers yes or no responses
	Can name objects
List items	Offers one- to two-word responses
What is this? And what is this? (point to different items; repeat)	Shows comprehension by following directions
(Items: ball, trees, shoes, sweatshirt, girl, ground, sky)	
Categorize or sequence objects/pictures	
Put these items in the same groups. You decide how to group them. Tell me about your grouping.	

Beginning interactive techniques parallel the same level of questions addressed earlier. Interactive techniques can engage more than one student at a time to facilitate small-group observations. Encouraging students to show understanding with gestures is a pre-linguistic activity that allows them to communicate before they know the correct words.

If, for example, an ELL is silent, giving directions invites gestures that show understanding, such as pointing to identify a picture. This is a non-verbal language behavior that indicates understanding, or a lack of understanding, depending on where the student points.

Initial language behaviors include yes or no responses and one-word responses. If a student can respond with a yes or no, he or she may include a pointing gesture as reinforcement. If the student can name items in a picture, an appropriate interactive technique is to list as many items as possible. Listing items, which is an appropriate language behavior for this level, allows ELLs to name things without worrying about making up complete sentences. Further, categorizing of pictures or objects allows students to show a deeper level of understanding. They are not just naming items but showing their relationships and, if possible, coming up with new words to label categories. The level does not require full sentence explanations, just labeling with single words or phrases.

Now let's look at some early intermediate techniques (Figure 3.9, below).

Small-Group Strategy: Color-Coded Responses
When asking students to list the items they see in a picture, record their answers on a piece of chart paper for all to see. Use colored markers to list the items each student can name. Assign a color to each student so that his or her responses are recorded in the corresponding color for easy identification. This allows the teacher to go back to the chart paper to see who said what without having to note a name to identify each response.

Figure 3.9 Level 2: Early Intermediate Techniques and Behaviors

Interactive Techniques	Student Behaviors
Identify essential features	Speaks in simple sentences
Tell me what you see in this picture.	Retells story events
What else do you see?	Reads basic vocabulary, simple
Retell events	sentences
	Makes frequent grammatical errors in
	speech

The interactive technique is very similar. It directs the student to talk about the picture, thus opening up space to say as much as possible. Open-ended conversations give insight into the variety of language behaviors used and the kinds of frequent errors or error patterns ELLs demonstrate. For instance, repeating such set phrases as "I see a dog. I see a cat. I see a cow" is language behavior typical of the early intermediate stage. Further, if you notice that a student makes frequent errors, such as "The _girl she kick_ the ball," you have an indication of what to teach with regard to noun and verb usage.

ELLs often tend to give a single answer and stop. In a small-group setting, the teacher can encourage students to keep talking by asking "What else do you see?"

Figure 3.10 (below) shows sample intermediate techniques.

Small-Group Strategy: Rehearse with a Partner

English language learners may be reluctant to speak in front of a class or even a small group. If you ask the students to share their words with a partner first as a form of rehearsal, it reduces their anxiety. Having them rehearse their responses does not skew the observation, because the teacher can listen in to what is said the first and second time. You can reasonably expect what they say will be very similar each time because ELLs at this level use a limited range of vocabulary and grammatical structures. With any developmental process such as language development, it is virtually impossible to simulate knowing how to say more than what is developed to this point. In other words, they can't fake it. They know what to say or they don't.

Figure 3.10 Level 3: Intermediate Techniques and Behaviors

Interactive Techniques	Student Behaviors
Encourage inquiry	Retells using expanded vocabulary
What do you want to know?	Identifies main ideas/details
What questions do you have?	Can summarize
Expand descriptive details	Makes comparisons
Tell me more about that. Add some details.	Defines new vocabulary
Can you say that in a different way?	
Explain in writing	
Can you write about what you see?	
Please share it with me.	

This is an appropriate stage to ask students to form their own questions. Encourage students to inquire. Note to what extent they formulate questions. Consider how many different kinds of questions they utilize. Are they all "what" questions? Or do they ask "where," "why," "which," and "how"?

A significant difference between levels 2 and 3 is the expanded use of oral and written language. Teachers can expect students at level 3 to embellish what they are describing by inserting adjectives and adverbs. For example, look for one or more adjectives in a sentence: "The big, blue car drove by."

This is also the level where it is appropriate to have students write their thoughts down. The amount of writing they produce provides one form of information, but look for the expanded use of adjectival and even adverbial phrases.

When children first learn to spell, they tend to write the same high frequency words over and over. It is not unusual to see a student write the following: "I like red. I like blue. I like red shoes. I like . . ." Consequently, the greater part of the writing may be spelled conventionally, but their word selection is narrow. On the other hand, a student with few inhibitions about conventions might write extensively and make a greater number of errors. Therefore, I suggest that spelling be part of a different type of assessment and that the writing sample be assessed only for expanded use of language without focusing on how words are spelled at this time.

Now let's move on to early intermediate techniques as shown in Figure 3.11 (below).

Small-Group Strategy: Collect a Written Paraphrase for Assessment

A quick, easy way to collect a writing sample from a student is to ask a group of students to pause and write a paraphrase of what they've learned or what they are thinking or what the group was discussing. Students writing in their own words provide authentic, unedited writing samples that can be assessed. The exercise does not have to be elaborate, but ask students to write several sentences about their thinking. It is an appropriate use of meta-cognitive thinking and benefits each student. I recommend setting an egg timer to two minutes to keep students focused on writing. Have students write in a journal, a double-entry journal, or on a half-sheet of paper for easy collection. The value of a journal is that the teacher has an ongoing record of writing samples. A double-entry journal provides context for the entry because the student would note in the left column what this entry was about (citations or labels) and in the right column would be the paraphrased entry. Using a half-sheet of paper for a paraphrased quick write is an easy way to manage and collect a writing sample. Also be sure to date the entry and include the student's name.

Figure 3.11 Level 4: Early Advanced Techniques and Questions

Interactive Technique	Student Behaviors
Solve problems	Appears to be orally fluent
What would you do . . . ?	Uses limited academic vocabulary and
How would you . . . ?	language
Picture yourself in the photograph. What	Needs to attain grade level reading and
would you be doing?	writing in academic areas

At the early advanced stage, posing a problem to solve invites a wide range of language behaviors. While solving a problem in a small-group setting, participants must pose questions, provide rationales for their thinking, argue their positions, define terms, and present their work to others.

Problem posing can take place in any subject area from literature and art to science and math. Having students imagine how a scene would change if a new character was inserted or imagine an alternative ending to a story poses problems to solve. Considering how to create a work of art in the style of Matisse is a problem. In science, deciding how to classify various plants or comparing the life cycles of butterflies to moths is best taught in a problem-solving mode. Math instruction increases the use of language when problem posing is employed, such as deciding on the best use of space in a small room.

In observing and assessing English language learners in a problem-solving situation, the teacher should be attentive to the ways students use language. Consider to what extent an ELL poses questions to others in the group. Does the ELL ask "why" and "how" questions of others? Does the ELL provide a clear rationale for his or her thinking? Consider to what extent the ELL is willing to present the results of the group to the rest of the class.

Finally, let's look at some advanced techniques and behaviors (Figure 3.12, below).

Small-Group Strategy: Problem-Solving Pods

When using a problem-solving approach, having a simple structure for roles and responsibilities ensures full participation by all. For example, when teaching a math problem, I recommend organizing the class into pods of three students. Each student has one of the following responsibilities: (1) language, (2) graphics, (3) calculations. Once the entire class is organized into pods, the teacher introduces the problem to be solved. Students are provided with materials such as a large sheet of graph paper, writing tools, and drawing tools. The teacher then invites the students in charge of language to receive instruction about the language of the problem, key words and definitions, and how to write about the problem. They are then sent to their pods to teach their peers. Next, the teacher invites the students who are in charge of graphics to discuss how to visually represent the problem and possible solutions; then they return to their pods to teach their peers. The students in charge of calculations are taught about numbers and functions to use to solve the problem. The teacher spends the balance of the time assisting, posing considerations, and observing language and problem-solving behaviors. Finally, each small group shares its processes and results and displays its work for evaluation. Students compare and decide on the best way to write about the problem, represent it visually, and calculate a result.

Figure 3.12 Level 5: Advanced Techniques and Behaviors

Interactive Techniques	Student Behaviors
Take leadership in collaborative groups	Comprehends content material
Please guide the discussion about the picture.	Generates discussions
	Is socially comfortable
Synthesize what others have said.	Reads and writes at grade level
In your own words, describe what the group discussed.	
Can you sum up what each person said? (May be oral or written.)	

One indicator of an English language learner at an advanced stage of language proficiency is the ability to use language in complex ways to perform a task such as guiding a discussion and synthesizing what a group has just discussed.

Small-Group Strategy: Utilize a Group Liaison

An efficient way to manage small groups is to appoint, or have students select, group liaisons. The role of a liaison is to represent a group to the teacher. Sometimes when working with multiple small groups in a classroom, the teacher can be overwhelmed by students' individual demands. If a group has a liaison, then the teacher speaks directly to the liaison, who conveys questions and needs to the teacher. In contrast, the teacher conveys direction and conferences with the liaison. This arrangement challenges the liaison to synthesize the messages from the group and puts the student into a small-group leadership role.

Using the CALL Record Sheet

Some teachers are happy to just make a copy of the CALL for each student and mark up the form with, for example, X's across the boxes over language level and stage and circles around key language behaviors, questions, interactive techniques, and differentiated strategies. The teacher can write the student's name on the CALL, date it, and place it in the student's file. Maintaining a record sheet provides the added benefit of recording progress in language development over time and providing comparative information of how an ELL is progressing throughout the academic year in relation to other ELL classmates.

The CALL Record Sheet (Figure 3.13, page 41) is a recording tool that is organized to note essential information about English language learners for each quarter of an academic year. It is a six-columned record sheet that includes a place to record the ELL's name and grade level, the date of each quarterly assessment, a specific language behavior that indicated the language level assessment, and a recommended differentiated strategy to apply. Each CALL Record Sheet can accommodate the assessment data for up to four English language learners for an entire academic year. Note that the CALL Record Sheet is also available as a Free Download on Eye On Education's website (see page xi).

Figure 3.14 (page 42) shows how to record information on the CALL Record Sheet. Note that a fifth grader named José Lopez was assessed in the first quarter of the academic year on 9/15/13. He was assessed as at level 2, early intermediate stage. A key language behavior that indicated that particular assessment was that he was able to orally summarize a text. In response, the teacher recommended two appropriate strategies to highlight for José: to teach study skills and to have him use and create media.

Let's think about those strategic instructional choices for a moment in light of José's language behavior. Being able to summarize a simple text is a language development strength for this student; it is also important for all students as a

Figure 3.13 Classroom Assessment of Language Levels (CALL) Record Sheet

Name/Grade Level	Key	1st Quarter	2nd Quarter	3rd Quarter	4th Quarter
	Level/Stage	Date:	Date:	Date:	Date:
	Language Behavior				
	Strategies				
	Level/Stage	Date:	Date:	Date:	Date:
	Language Behavior				
	Strategies				
	Level/Stage	Date:	Date:	Date:	Date:
	Language Behavior				
	Strategies				
	Level/Stage	Date:	Date:	Date:	Date:
	Language Behavior				
	Strategies				

Figure 3.14 Example of the CALL Record Sheet

Name/Grade Level	Key	1st Quarter	2nd Quarter
Lopez, José 5th Grade	Level/ Stage	2/Early Intermed. Date: 9/15/13	3/Intermed. Date: 12/18/13
	Language Behavior	Summarizes texts	Retells using expanded vocabulary
	Strategies	Teach study skills Use-create media	Explore word origins
	Level/ Stage	Date:	Date:

study skill. By highlighting teaching study skills, the teacher chose to build on his language strength and teach something that would benefit a wide range of students in the class. This highly appropriate strategy for an ELL at this stage of language development is an easy way to differentiate while accommodating a maximum number of students in class.

The other strategy that the teacher plans to employ is to have the student use and create media. Although very little detail is recorded on the CALL Record Sheet, there is enough to note that the ELL will engage in some form of project-based learning using and creating media. Again, based upon the key language behavior, the teacher will ensure that some component of the media-based project will involve summarizing a text. This is a natural strategy for a wide-range of media projects, such as using presentation software to summarize essential information from a textbook chapter, using digital storytelling to summarize a lengthy story, editing an interview with an expert about a particular topic, or creating a PDF for the rest of the class with essential information from a research report. In each case, the use and creation of media required the skill of summarizing a text of some sort.

The teacher would follow up with José during each of the subsequent quarters of the academic year. The form allows for flexibility with regard to the specific date of the next assessment. Setting a date to assess each ELL each quarter may have the benefit of establishing a regular routine of assessment in the classroom. On the negative side, it can also create an arbitrary deadline that may force a teacher to conduct an assessment at an inopportune time in the instructional calendar. Another approach is to maintain observational vigilance of the ELLs as you teach the class. When something noteworthy occurs, such as a demonstration of language behavior above a student's current level, the teacher may plan to conduct an assessment. The benefit of this other approach is to establish a more organic cycle of assessment/instruction/assessment/ instruction on an as-needed basis.

A final note about the CALL Record Sheet is the component of duration on the CALL itself. As stated earlier, the duration that an ELL remains at a particular stage is somewhat predictable when other supporting factors are in place. Those predictable periods of time are provided on the CALL. Supporting factors include family support, literacy in the primary language, cognitive processing ability, socioeconomic status, the school environment, and the quality of the instruction provided. Over time, if a teacher begins to record little or no progress for a student, there is cause to look at supporting factors for language development. To address a lack of progress, a teacher may begin to look at the quality of his or her instruction and the school environment and/or call for a conference with the parents or guardians. If more intervention is needed, as in the case of cognitive processing ability, the record sheet may be used as one piece of evidence to call for a student support team (SST) meeting to further assess what is going on with a particular student.

Part 2

Classroom Strategies for ELLs at Each Level

4

Level 1: The Beginning Stage and Common Core Listening and Speaking

This chapter provides an in-depth look at the language behaviors and appropriate teaching strategies and activities for beginning level English language learners. The strategies and activities align with the Common Core State Standards for Listening and Speaking according to the following grade level ranges: K–2, 3–5, 6–8, and 9–12.

Starting from Silence

Level 1, the beginning stage, is characterized by a silent period in which the ELL is actively listening and acquiring basic oral language to communicate minimally. The silence can be perplexing to inexperienced classroom teachers who want to immediately engage their students with multiple questions, expecting to hear responses, but just receive timid stares in return. This is the beginning of the journey from silence to utterances to literacy to proficiency. It takes time to become proficient in another language. Like any long journey, it begins with those first tentative steps. Students at this stage predictably exhibit the following types of language related behaviors:

- Can be silent
- Offers yes/no responses
- Can name objects
- Offers 1- to 2-word responses
- Shows comprehension by following directions

The Beginning Stage English Language Learner

To understand the characteristics and appropriate strategies for beginning level English language learners, imagine going on a trip to a country where you don't speak the native language. When you step off the airplane, you hear the hustle and bustle of the airport, but much of it may sound like noise, rather than comprehensible speech. Out of necessity, you rely less on your ears than on your eyes. Pre-linguistic clues are what guide you. You look for signs with pictures that show you where to get your luggage and ground transportation. You follow the gestures of the staff directing you the right way to find your bags. You find the right bathroom, not because of the lettering on the door indicating men or women but because you see and understand the universal images, a female in a skirt or a generic male apparently in pants (Figure 4.1, page 49). The words with the pictures are simply abstract markings to you at this point of your language development. Visuals and meaningful gestures are your primary means of communication.

You are able to indicate understanding by nodding your head for yes or shaking your head for no. You may also use gestures, such as raising your shoulders toward your ears and lifting your arms at the elbows with palms up to indicate "I don't know" (Figure 4.2, page 49).

The reality is that when you step off an airplane, as a new arrival in a country where you don't speak the language, you have a limited range of ability to communicate, and you are probably feeling a little anxious about being in new and unfamiliar surroundings. The communication is characterized by a combination of gestures, signs, and the occasional word or two, such as a greeting or a yes or no response. It is as though someone changed your world around and switched all the labels. You recognize things, but you don't have the words to name them. But even though you don't feel particularly smart at this level, you haven't lost your intelligence. I make this point because teachers often treat beginning ELLs as if they aren't smart. On the contrary, beginning language learners are extremely attentive to their surroundings because they are actively looking for comprehensible clues.

Intense, active listening is a key characteristic of beginning ELLs. They have a wide-eyed quality, and they look for meaning in every facet of the day. In fact, the intensity of the listening and searching for understandable messages can at times be overwhelming. It is not at all uncommon for English language learners to fall asleep after a couple of hours in a classroom. The nonstop scrutiny of what is going on about them causes sheer exhaustion. Uninformed teachers often misinterpret ELLs' falling asleep in class as disrespectful behavior. An uninformed teacher will react by raising her or his voice and berating the unsuspecting new arrival with a barrage of high volume, fast-paced speech. Consider how unhelpful that is. First, the ELL may be confused about what is wrong or why the teacher is angry. Second, fast-paced speech will predictably be entirely incomprehensible to the ELL. Finally, raising one's voice to make a point falsely implies that the ELL has a hearing disorder rather than limited language proficiency. Raising your volume of speech will only create anxiety and inhibit instruction. A better

Figure 4.1 Toilet
Sign in Mandarin

Figure 4.2 Gesturing
"I don't know."

approach is to recognize that active and intense listening for meaning is fostered by providing visually rich instruction in smaller time segments broken up by group activities and individual time to work at a more relaxed pace. If a student falls asleep, recognize that it is involuntary and that the student is exhausted.

When I teach pre-service teachers, I like to show them a video of a kindergarten classroom from Beijing, China, in which students are being taught in Mandarin. I don't tell the aspiring teachers the subject being taught. I ask them to imagine that they are newly arrived students in the classroom. As we view the classroom from the eye of a language learner, I ask them to consider what the teacher does that is *helpful* to make sense of the learning. I also ask them to note when they don't understand what is going on in the classroom; in other words, what does the teacher do that is *unhelpful* for comprehension.

Invariably, my pre-service teacher candidates point out that the use of visuals and meaningful gestures were helpful strategies that allowed them to comprehend that they were watching a math lesson on combining doubles (1 + 1 = 2, 2 + 2 = 4, and so forth). In contrast, they are quick to point out that when the teacher provided long explanations without the use of visuals, they were completely lost, and the instruction was meaningless. I show them only a couple of minutes of the video, even though I have the entire 45-minute class recorded. Because of the intensity of their active listening, they can focus for only a few minutes before their attention wanes.

Figure 4.3 (page 50) summarizes helpful and unhelpful practices for beginning English language learners.

Something else I ask my pre-service teacher candidates to imagine while viewing the Beijing classroom video is how they might feel during the segment when the teacher calls exclusively on individual students who raise their hands. She then invites them come to the front of the classroom to announce the correct answer, and she praises their intelligence because they are right!

As the pre-service teacher candidates put themselves in the shoes of a newly arrived beginning language learner, they express a sense of anxiety, hoping that they will not be called upon. People generally avoid putting their ignorance on display in front of a group of peers, so it makes sense to reduce those kinds of situations in the classroom. Rather than putting ELLs on the spot in front of the class, consider alternative ways to respond to the learning, such as giving students the opportunity to talk with a partner or in a small group to rehearse an answer to a question before risking addressing the entire class.

Figure 4.3 Helpful Strategies and Unhelpful Practices for Beginning ELLs

Helpful Strategies	Unhelpful Practices
Showing visuals and real objects that give clues and images about the instruction	Providing lengthy explanations without visual clues or realia
Actively engaging all students in meaningful gestures that contribute to understanding	Expecting students to endure long periods of passive listening without active involvement
Providing short, targeted instruction followed by active responses	Calling only on selected individuals to announce correct answers to the entire class
Using small-group sharing to rehearse answers before raising hands to address the entire class	Providing only one way to respond to questions
Using response boards	

Recommended Strategies for Beginning English Language Learners Defined

The following strategies are appropriate across grade levels; however, they may look different within specific grade ranges. This section defines each strategy in detail. The following section provides specific instructional examples of the strategies as they apply to the grade ranges of elementary, middle, and high school.

◆ Employ simple "caretaker" speech
◆ Use realia and visuals
◆ Show meaning with gestures and Total Physical Response (TPR)
◆ Avoid forced speech
◆ Select attractive books and read with students

Employ Simple "Caretaker" Speech

There are several components to take into account: pacing and emphasis, volume, and word choice.

Generally, pacing refers to the speed at which a person speaks. Emphasis is the stress and attention given to selected words. It is highly recommended that teachers slow down when they speak. However, pacing also includes varying speeds to increase interest. Sometimes, it may mean speeding up the pace in order to be able to slow down when emphasizing a particular word. When key words come up, take time to emphasize or highlight the words. Draw out the pronunciation and even indicate with a gesture that you are emphasizing a word.

Volume of speech can establish an appropriate tone for learning or generate undue anxiety and confusion. As mentioned above, when a teacher raises his or her voice at a student, it is open to misinterpretation and can have the unintended consequences of engendering fear of the classroom setting. Regulating volume requires cultural insight. For example, Mexican males rarely raise their voices, except in extreme emergency situations. A loud teacher can have the effect of setting an instructional tone that would be perceived as a constant emergency situation. On the other hand, Argentinian males are much more demonstrative and might not feel stressed in a louder classroom setting. Generally, a good initial practice is for teachers to refrain from raising their voices in class. However, the lesson here is to be attentive to the best volume for the students. Think of it as tuning in to their frequency. A good gauge for volume is to have a friendly conversation with the parents to see if they are soft spoken or louder and more demonstrative. In class, try the following experiment: while the class is working in groups and generating good collaborative, instructional noise, in a soft voice say, "Class, look at me. I want your attention." See which students immediately look up. Try it a second time, but say it more softly. See if the same students look up or if more students attend. At other times, try using different volume levels to get students to look up at you. This will indicate the speaking level you need to use so the whole group will tune in. In time, a teacher will identify an appropriate volume to use for instruction with a given group of English language learners. When teaching a mixed group of students, vary the use of volume for strategic purposes. Give directions in a soft voice and check for understanding. Raise or lower the volume if needed.

The final component of "caretaker" speech is word choice. At the elementary level, simpler words are your best choice when communicating with beginning language learners. Keep sentences short. Using predictable word patterns helps as well. At the upper elementary and secondary levels, word choice becomes more focused on the use of cognates. Cognates are those words that have a common linguistic or etymological origin. Of course, languages with Latin and/ or Greek origins will have more cognates with English than Asian languages. Nevertheless, skilled use of cognates increases understanding, particularly in content area instruction.

Use Realia and Visuals

Whenever possible, the most efficient way to communicate a meaningful message to an ELL is to show realia (real objects, models, actual experiences, dramatizations) and visuals (pictures, video, flow charts, drawings). Use of realia is more meaningful than showing visuals because real objects tap multiple senses of touch, sight, sound, smell, and even taste. Words alone are abstractions of realia; visuals are representational. I can say the word "*fuji*," but until I show you an apple or a picture of a Mountain in Japan, you may not know what I am talking about. The key strategy is to show first, and then label the realia or picture with the target vocabulary word. Consider if I show a native of Japan a picture of Mount Fuji. Before a word is said, the meaning is conveyed. The image is meaningful at a representational, pre-linguistic level. Then I label it with the word "mountain" in English, and now the word makes sense. If I try to begin with an abstract word, I create confusion. In the same way, imagine if I showed you a word card with Japanese characters written on it; unless you knew the language the characters would be abstract and meaningless to you. You would need to see something meaningful first. Therefore, show first; label second.

Show Meaning with Gestures and Total Physical Response (TPR)

James Asher (1977) coined the term "Total Physical Response," using meaningful gestures and actions to teach language. I will provide specific examples of TPR later on in the book; but, to illustrate TPR, picture a teacher leaping in the air with her students to teach the word "jump," or molding clay into a geometric shape to teach the word "trapezoid." Total Physical Response is not like the game "Simon Says" in the sense that the teacher is trying to trap students or catch them making an error. It is like the game in the sense that everyone is moving and gesturing to commands that meaningfully represent targeted vocabulary.

Avoid Forced Speech

Occasionally, I have witnessed frustrated classroom teachers insist that their students "Speak English!" as if they actually could. It would be like me insisting that you speak Latvian. Imagine me ordering an English-only speaker to "Speak Latvian!" It makes no sense and only scares people who don't understand the language. The only message that is conveyed by this ludicrous command to speak English "now" is that the teacher is angry for an incomprehensible reason. Students at the beginning stages most likely will not understand the command and just become afraid to speak at all, thus creating the opposite effect of the command.

Select Attractive Books and Read with Students

I love to say that literacy begins with a juicy story. Select books that will captivate students' imaginations and provide a rich lexicon of words to learn. Help students see and hear the language with gorgeous books that are vividly illustrated. Read to students. Show the relationship between the words on the page and illustrations in the book. Model how words are pronounced. Enjoy a juicy story together; it is one of life's great pleasures.

Common Core State Standards for Listening and Speaking and Beginning English Language Learners

This section provides specific examples of how to apply the strategies within the following grade ranges: K–2 (Figure 4.4) and 3–5 (elementary school) (Figure 4.5), 6–8 (middle school) (Figure 4.7), and 9–12 (high school) (Figure 4.8). Although the suggested strategies are applicable across grade levels, they will look different within grade ranges. The following examples at each grade range demonstrate the unique features of instruction and accommodation using the suggested strategies. Additionally, the following section is intended to be exemplary rather than comprehensive. To cover all Common Core State Standards would involve writing another book on the subject. However, I've included all of the Listening and Speaking Common Core State Standards in the following figures (I added the bold emphasis). At this point, the Common Core State Standards are not differentiated according to language levels. Though the focus of this chapter is the beginning stage, each of the following chapters is dedicated to a subsequent stage of language development and provides specific strategies and activities for each language level.

Note to Readers: If you are a middle-school teacher, you may wish to skip ahead to your grade range at this point.

Figure 4.4 Common Core State Standards for Listening and Speaking: K–2

Kindergarten	1. Participate in collaborative conversations with diverse partners about *kindergarten topics and texts* with peers and adults in small and larger groups. a) Follow agreed-upon rules for discussions (e.g., listening to others and taking turns speaking about the topics and texts under discussion). b) Continue a conversation through multiple exchanges. 2. Confirm understanding of a text read aloud or information presented orally or through other media by asking and answering questions about key details and requesting clarification if something is not understood. **a) Understand and follow one- and two-step oral directions.** 3. Ask and answer questions in order to seek help, get information, or clarify something that is not understood.
Grade 1	1. Participate in collaborative conversations with diverse partners about *grade 1 topics and texts* with peers and adults in small and larger groups. a) Follow agreed-upon rules for discussions (e.g., listening to others with care, speaking one at a time about the topics and texts under discussion). b) Build on others' talk in conversations by responding to the comments of others through multiple exchanges. c) Ask questions to clear up any confusion about the topics and texts under discussion. 2. Ask and answer questions about key details in a text read aloud or information presented orally or through other media. **a) Give, restate, and follow simple two-step directions.** 3. Ask and answer questions about what a speaker says in order to gather additional information or clarify something that is not understood.
Grade 2	1. Participate in collaborative conversations with diverse partners about *grade 2 topics and texts* with peers and adults in small and larger groups. a) Follow agreed-upon rules for discussions (e.g., gaining the floor in respectful ways, listening to others with care, speaking one at a time about the topics and texts under discussion). b) Build on others' talk in conversations by linking their comments to the remarks of others. c) Ask for clarification and further explanation as needed about the topics and texts under discussion. 2. Recount or describe key ideas or details from a text read aloud or information presented orally or through other media. **a) Give and follow three- and four-step oral directions.** 3. Ask and answer questions about what a speaker says in order to clarify comprehension, gather additional information, or deepen understanding of a topic or issue.

Strategies for Comprehension and Collaboration, Grades K–2

Model Meaningful Gestures and Simple Questions

♦ Model for beginning English language learners a set of meaningful gestures to participate in a discussion, such as the following:
Thumbs up—yes, or I understand
Thumbs sideways—I'm not sure
Thumbs down—no, or I don't understand
♦ Use Total Physical Response (www.tpr-world.com) to model acting out the actions of a text. Write the TPR commands on a large sheet of chart paper. Number each one for quick reference. Have the students take turns leading the group in the commands.
♦ Provide an advanced organizer with pictures to represent each topic, theme, or question to discuss.
♦ Teach simple clarification requests and questions: "Please repeat." "What did you say?" "Show me, please."

Illustrate Details with a Storyboard

Have students draw up a storyboard that sequences the key ideas or details of the text. Cut the storyboard into individual pictures to mix up and rearrange in order.

Identify Character Details from Storyboard Illustrations

♦ Ask students to point to the part in the illustration that answers the questions: "Point to the boy who is chasing the dog."
♦ Use either/or questions that embed the answer in the question for the student: "Was the boy <u>running</u> or was he <u>walking</u> ?"
♦ Use fill-in-the-blank questions to allow students to respond with a single answer: "José chased after his _____ . (pet, dog, or cat)"

Figure 4.5 Common Core State Standards for Listening and Speaking: Grades 3–5

Grade 3	1. Engage effectively in a range of collaborative discussions (one-on-one, in groups, and teacher-led) with diverse partners on *grade 3 topics and texts*, building on others' ideas and expressing their own clearly. a) Come to discussions prepared, having read or studied required material; explicitly draw on that preparation and other information known about the topic to explore ideas under discussion. b) Follow agreed-upon rules for discussions (e.g., gaining the floor in respectful ways, listening to others with care, speaking one at a time about the

topics and texts under discussion). c) Ask questions to check understanding of information presented, stay on topic, and link their comments to the remarks of others. d) Explain their own ideas and understanding in light of the discussion.

2. Determine the main ideas and supporting details of a text read aloud or information presented in diverse media and formats, including visually, quantitatively, and orally.

3. Ask and answer questions about information from a speaker, offering appropriate elaboration and detail.

Grade 4

1. Engage effectively in a range of collaborative discussions (one-on-one, in groups, and teacher-led) with diverse partners on *grade 4 topics and texts*, building on others' ideas and expressing their own clearly. a) Come to discussions prepared, having read or studied required material; explicitly draw on that preparation and other information known about the topic to explore ideas under discussion. b) Follow agreed-upon rules for discussions and carry out assigned roles. c) Pose and respond to specific questions to clarify or follow up on information, and make comments that contribute to the discussion and link to the remarks of others. d) Review the key ideas expressed and explain their own ideas and understanding in light of the discussion.

2. Paraphrase portions of a text read aloud or information presented in diverse media and formats, including visually, quantitatively, and orally.

3. Identify the reasons and evidence a speaker **or media source** provides to support particular points.

Grade 5

1. Engage effectively in a range of collaborative discussions (one-on-one, in groups, and teacher-led) with diverse partners on *grade 5 topics and texts*, building on others' ideas and expressing their own clearly. a) Come to discussions prepared, having read or studied required material; explicitly draw on that preparation and other information known about the topic to explore ideas under discussion. b) Follow agreed-upon rules for discussions and carry out assigned roles. c) Pose and respond to specific questions by making comments that contribute to the discussion and elaborate on the remarks of others. d) Review the key ideas expressed and draw conclusions in light of information and knowledge gained from the discussions.

2. Summarize a written text read aloud or information presented in diverse media and formats, including visually, quantitatively, and orally.

3. Summarize the points a speaker **or media source** makes and explain how each claim is supported by reasons and evidence, **and identify and analyze any logical fallacies.**

Strategies for Comprehension and Collaboration, Grades 3–5

Provide Primary Language (L₁) Support with Preview/Review

◆ Preview/review in the primary language is the most efficient way to address this standard with a level 1 student. In multilingual classroom settings, this poses challenges. It requires that students have dual-language dictionaries or access to Internet-based dictionaries in the students' languages.
◆ Preview the key vocabulary and major points of the lesson. Pair up students according to language groupings. Ask students to find the words in their primary language dictionaries and to discuss the topic of the lesson in their home languages.
◆ Teach the lesson in English with the use of visuals and graphic organizers.
◆ Review the lesson in small language groups. Encourage students to discuss the key ideas in their own languages and to illustrate the learning.

Provide Bit-Sized Chunks of Text

◆ Organize a text into meaningful parts. Assign small groups to illustrate and paraphrase the meanings of selected passages. Then share the illustrated paraphrases with the rest of the class. Each group contributes to the whole text.
◆ With mathematical texts, organize students into small groups of three and assign each student a role: illustrator, paraphraser, and calculator. Invite students responsible for each role to meet and discuss key points. Offer advice about what students should share with their groups. For example, call the illustrators together and discuss what should be in the picture; then call all the paraphrasers together to discuss key words, spelling, and phrasing of the text. Finally, call the calculators together to discuss

Figure 4.6 Sample Cluster Map for Organizing Main Idea

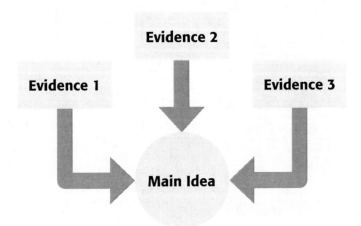

meaningful numbers and functions to use. Group members then teach their peers in the small groups. Each group produces an illustrated paraphrase with calculations from the text to share with the whole class.

Use Graphic Organizers to Show Relationships

Use graphic organizers to deconstruct a text into main idea and supporting evidence (see Figure 4.6 on page 56). A cluster map would work well for this standard. Encourage illustrations for each idea.

Figure 4.7 Common Core State Standards for Listening and Speaking: Grades 6–8

Grade 6	1. Engage effectively in a range of collaborative discussions (one-on-one, in groups, and teacher-led) with diverse partners on *grade 6 topics, texts, and issues*, building on others' ideas and expressing their own clearly. a) Come to discussions prepared, having read or studied required material; explicitly draw on that preparation by referring to evidence on the topic, text, or issue to probe and reflect on ideas under discussion. b) Follow rules for collegial discussions, set specific goals and deadlines, and define individual roles as needed. c) Pose and respond to specific questions with elaboration and detail by making comments that contribute to the topic, text, or issue under discussion. d) Review the key ideas expressed and demonstrate understanding of multiple perspectives through reflection and paraphrasing. 2. Interpret information presented in diverse media and formats (e.g., visually, quantitatively, orally) and explain how it contributes to a topic, text, or issue under study. 3. Delineate a speaker's argument and specific claims, distinguishing claims that are supported by reasons and evidence from claims that are not.
Grade 7	1. Engage effectively in a range of collaborative discussions (one-on-one, in groups, and teacher-led) with diverse partners on *grade 7 topics, texts, and issues*, building on others' ideas and expressing their own clearly. a) Come to discussions prepared, having read or researched material under study; explicitly draw on that preparation by referring to evidence on the topic, text, or issue to probe and reflect on ideas under discussion. b) Follow rules for collegial discussions, track progress toward specific goals and deadlines, and define individual roles as needed. c) Pose questions that elicit elaboration and respond to others' questions and comments with relevant observations and ideas that bring the discussion back on topic as needed. d) Acknowledge new information expressed by others and, when warranted, modify their own views.

	2. Analyze the main ideas and supporting details presented in diverse media and formats (e.g., visually, quantitatively, orally) and explain how the ideas clarify a topic, text, or issue under study. 3. Delineate a speaker's argument and specific claims, **and attitude toward the subject,** evaluating the soundness of the reasoning and the relevance and sufficiency of the evidence.
Grade 8	1. Engage effectively in a range of collaborative discussions (one-on-one, in groups, and teacher-led) with diverse partners on *grade 8 topics, texts, and issues,* building on others' ideas and expressing their own clearly. a) Come to discussions prepared, having read or researched material under study; explicitly draw on that preparation by referring to evidence on the topic, text, or issue to probe and reflect on ideas under discussion. b) Follow rules for collegial discussions and decision-making, track progress toward specific goals and deadlines, and define individual roles as needed. c) Pose questions that connect the ideas of several speakers and respond to others' questions and comments with relevant evidence, observations, and ideas. d) Acknowledge new information expressed by others, and, when warranted, qualify or justify their own views in light of the evidence presented. 2. Analyze the purpose of information presented in diverse media and formats (e.g., visually, quantitatively, orally) and evaluate the motives (e.g., social, commercial, political) behind its presentation. 3. Delineate a speaker's argument and specific claims, evaluating the soundness of the reasoning and relevance and sufficiency of the evidence and identifying when irrelevant evidence is introduced.

Strategies for Comprehension and Collaboration, Grades 6–8

Apply Preview/Review with Discussion Protocols

(Please see the preview/review suggestion for grades 3, 4, and 5 on page 56. It applies here as well.)

◆ Explicitly teach and apply small-group *discussion protocols*:
  • Numbered heads—assigned turn taking
  • Think/pair/share—pairing students
  • Merry-go-round—everyone takes a short turn
  • Put in your two cents—controlled talk with tokens
  • Circle the sage—interview a person who has specialized knowledge.
◆ Teach set discussion phrases:
  • "What do you think . . . ? "
  • "Do we agree with that?"

- "What is the evidence?"
- "Is there another point of view?"
- "Do we agree?" "Do we disagree?"

For more information, see notebook.lausd.net/pls/ptl/docs/PAGE/ CA_LAUSD/LAUSDNET/ABOUT_US/INITIATIVES/AEMP/CAG_HOME/ PROFESSIONAL%20DEVELOPMENT/GLC%202%20PROTOCOLS.PDF.

Use Digital Cameras to Conduct a Neighborhood Study of Text Usage

Assign students to bring to class examples of text from their neighborhoods. Encourage digital photos of street signs, business postings, directions, and bumper stickers. Classify the examples according to format and motives. Post the pictures in their category groupings. Add to the posting throughout the school year. Include similar examples of text from class readings.

Set Up a Round-Robin Discussion

Conduct a round-robin discussion and deconstruction: Organize students into small groups, and give each group a passage of text that asserts a claim. On a single piece of paper, each group does one of the following tasks in order. After a task is performed, the group passes its work to another group so each group evaluates the work of the previous group. Do the following:

- Identify a speaker's claim.
- Cite the supporting evidence.
- Decide whether each piece of evidence is relevant to the claim.
- Evaluate the strength of the claim.

Figure 4.8 Common Core State Standards for Listening and Speaking: Grades 9–12

Note: Readers will see that the standards for high-school students are very similar from grade to grade with only minor differences. Further, the standards are multifaceted and complex. An English language learner at level 1, the beginning stage, cannot be expected to conduct high level discussions; however, the group can be asked to comply with the standards by establishing rules of conduct that invite the participation of an ELL. The group can utilize media sources to make discussion and interaction more comprehensible, and all learners can apply a simple evaluation rubric to their discussion.

Grades 9–10	1. Initiate and participate effectively in a range of collaborative discussions (one-on-one, in groups, and teacher-led) with diverse partners on *grades 9–10 topics, texts, and issues*, building on others' ideas and expressing their own clearly and persuasively. a) Come to discussions prepared, having read and researched material under study; explicitly draw on that preparation by referring to evidence from texts and other research on the topic or issue to stimulate a thoughtful,

well-reasoned exchange of ideas. b) Work with peers to set rules for collegial discussions and decision-making (e.g., informal consensus, taking votes on key issues, presentation of alternate views), clear goals and deadlines, and individual roles as needed. c) Propel conversations by posing and responding to questions that relate the current discussion to broader themes or larger ideas; actively incorporate others into the discussion; and clarify, verify, or challenge ideas and conclusions. d) Respond thoughtfully to diverse perspectives, summarize points of agreement and disagreement, and, when warranted, qualify or justify their own views and understanding and make new connections in light of the evidence and reasoning presented.

2. Integrate multiple sources of information presented in diverse media or formats (e.g., visually, quantitatively, orally) evaluating the credibility and accuracy of each source.

3. Evaluate a speaker's point of view, reasoning, and use of evidence and rhetoric, identifying any fallacious reasoning or exaggerated or distorted evidence.

| Grades 11–12 | 1. Initiate and participate effectively in a range of collaborative discussions (one-on-one, in groups, and teacher-led) with diverse partners on *grades 11–12 topics, texts, and issues*, building on others' ideas and expressing their own clearly and persuasively. a) Come to discussions prepared, having read and researched material under study; explicitly draw on that preparation by referring to evidence from texts and other research on the topic or issue to stimulate a thoughtful, well-reasoned exchange of ideas. b) Work with peers to promote civil, democratic discussions and decision-making, set clear goals and deadlines, and establish individual roles as needed. c) Propel conversations by posing and responding to questions that probe reasoning and evidence; ensure a hearing for a full range of positions on a topic or issue; clarify, verify, or challenge ideas and conclusions; and promote divergent and creative perspectives. d) Respond thoughtfully to diverse perspectives; synthesize comments, claims, and evidence made on all sides of an issue; resolve contradictions when possible; and determine what additional information or research is required to deepen the investigation or complete the task.

2. Integrate multiple sources of information presented in diverse formats and media (e.g., visually, quantitatively, orally) in order to make informed decisions and solve problems, evaluating the credibility and accuracy of each source and noting any discrepancies among the data.

3. Evaluate a speaker's point of view, reasoning, and use of evidence and rhetoric, assessing the stance, premises, links among ideas, word choice, points of emphasis, and tone used. |

Strategies for Comprehension and Collaboration, Grades 9–12

Establish Rules for Inclusive Discussions

Although the components of these standards require that English language learners function at a higher level of proficiency than beginning, small groups of students can be asked to establish rules of discussion that foster comprehension and collaboration with ELLs. Consider calling on students to establish rules for small-group discussion that include the following:

◆ Have participants sketch and illustrate their ideas on a response board.
◆ Include frequent checks for understanding or the need for clarification.
◆ Establish hand gestures such as thumbs-up (I agree or understand), thumbs-down (I disagree or don't understand), thumbs-sideways (I'm not sure).
◆ Include some use of yes and no and either/or questions to ensure participation of beginning stage ELLs.

Use Mixed Media, Realia, Visuals, and Models

Place a premium on highly visual interaction. Select and use short video clips to increase comprehension. Whenever possible, bring in actual objects to explore and examine. Encourage all students to sketch on response boards to illustrate their ideas. At times, make and display scale models of the object of study.

Encourage ELLs to Evaluate Speakers and Discussions with a Simple Rubric

To help a beginning English language learner participate in the evaluation of a speaker or discussion, use a simple rubric that is highly visual and numeric. The sample rubric in Figure 4.9 (page 62) facilitates conducting a brief evaluation of the quality of a speaker or discussion in terms of interaction, clear reasoning, and supporting evidence. I prefer a four-point scale:

4 = Exceeds criteria (Very clear reasoning and extensive supporting evidence)
3 = Meets criteria (Well-reasoned with sufficient supporting evidence)
2 = Below criteria (Lack of reasoning with little supporting evidence)
1 = Missing or off topic (Unclear or off topic reasoning without supporting evidence)

The general scale allows teachers to tailor the criteria for particular topics of discussion without having to change the rubric each time. The range challenges students to try to exceed the criteria. A four-point scale also forces the evaluator to take a stance on whether the speaker or discussion group did in fact meet criteria. There is no middle ground. The rubric is pictorial to increase comprehension at a glance. It is not highly text based in order to allow students at all language levels to participate in the evaluation process.

Figure 4.9 Illustrated Speaker or Discussion Rubric

Rubric	Exceeds Criteria	Meets Criteria	Below Criteria	Missing or Off Topic
Interactive	4	3	2	1
Clear Reasoning	4	3	2	1
Supporting Evidence	4	3	2	1

Source: Created by the author.

5

Level 2: The Early Intermediate Stage and Common Core Listening and Speaking

This chapter continues with an examination of the language behaviors and appropriate teaching strategies and activities for level 2, early intermediate stage, English language learners. This stage marks the shift from silence and single-phrase utterances at the beginning stage to speaking initial narratives with frequent errors. The strategies and activities align with the Common Core Standards for Listening and Speaking according to the following grade level ranges: K–2, 3–5, 6–8, and 9–12.

Emergent Literacy

Although the early intermediate stage identifies marked changes in ELL's language behaviors, stages are really abstractions of the reality of language development (Purcell-Gates, 2004). They are not necessarily clearly defined divisions. Language development moves in phases characterized by marked advancement, minor improvement or stationary progress, regression, and then advancement again. At times, ELLs will demonstrate significant progress in speaking simple sentences, indicating behaviors at the early intermediate stage. Predictably, there will be times of little evidence of improving language proficiency as the ELLs establish fluency with current learning. At other times, ELLs may be in unfamiliar circumstances and regress to silence for a period of time, using single phrases before speaking in sentences again. The tension of regression can also motivate ELLs to learn more and begin to exhibit marked improvement again. This back

Figure 5.1 Factors to Consider for Long Term ELLs

Level of oral language proficiency in the first language (L_1)
Level of print literacy proficiency (L_1)
Environmental factors, such as home literacy and access to print material
More-complex vocabulary in a wide range of new topics and instructional
   content areas
The onset of reading in a new language
The onset of writing in a new language

Source: Olsen, L. (2010). *Reparable harm: Fulfilling the unkept promise of educational opportunity for California's long term English Learners.* Long Beach, CA: Californians Together. November 22, 2010, from http://www.californianstogether.org/docs/download.aspx?fileId=12

and forth movement of progression, stasis, regression, and progression again is quite natural and expected. Over time, and with quality teaching that provides linguistic supports, one can expect ELLs to move through this stage in due course.

Be aware that ELLs tend to linger in the early intermediate and intermediate stages longer than any of the other stages for a number of reasons. ELLs can remain at this stage for anywhere from three months to a year. Multiple factors comprise what happens at this stage. Consider the difference between two ELLs: one may have been well schooled in the primary language (L_1), or home language, prior to learning English; another ELL may be just learning to read in any language. Therefore, a major factor in how long an ELL remains at the early intermediate and intermediate stages is the level of oral and print literacy development the child has in the primary language. Another factor is to what extent a child's home environment fosters literacy development. At this stage, in addition to developing oral fluency across a wider range of topics, ELLs begin to develop print literacy with reading and writing in various genres and styles. This is a tremendous undertaking in any language. To develop proficiency in oral fluency, reading, and expressive writing requires quality, active participation over time in all three aspects of literacy development.

Figure 5.1 (above) shows the factors that contribute to extended time at the early intermediate and intermediate stages of language development.

The Early Intermediate Stage English Language Learner

Identifiable language behaviors of a student at the early intermediate stage are as follows:

◆ Speaks in simple sentences
◆ Retells story events
◆ Reads basic vocabulary and simple sentences
◆ Makes frequent grammatical errors in speech

As stated previously, level 2 is characterized by initial attempts at telling narratives using simple sentences and making frequent errors. When I was a classroom teacher, occasionally an ELL would run up to me on the playground and begin to complain about another student's behavior—someone had cheated or mistreated a friend. The student would use simple sentences, such as, "He *cheat* me." Or "She *say* a bad word." The sentences were short and often grammatically incorrect but could include noun and verb phrases of the student's construction. At times, instead of directly addressing the student's concerns, I would shake his or her hand and say, "Congratulations! You've just attained early intermediate fluency." Needless to say, this unexpected response would leave the student quite perplexed, but the demonstration of a marked shift from isolated words to simple narratives indicated a level of literacy being attained.

Imagine again that you are traveling in a foreign country. You've been there a while and can navigate your way through the day with a set of survival phrases. You know how to order a room in a hotel. You can tell a taxi driver where to take you. And you can order familiar items from a menu at a restaurant you frequent. You probably know the words associated with money exchange, days of the week, and how to greet new friends on the street. You've also learned to ask "What is that?" or "What does that mean?" As you drive around the city in a taxi, however, you see some familiar signs, but others, you cannot decipher. You might recognize every letter and could accurately pronounce the words but not understand what they mean. I recall being in Guatemala and seeing signs for *viveros*. I figured that it had something to do with living things because I knew the root-word *vivir* (to live), but that was all I could ascertain. It took a visit to the site to understand that *viveros* referred to plant nurseries. In other words, letter recognition did not make the word meaningful. I needed a meaningful experience to be able to read and understand the word on the signpost.

This anecdote reveals an important axiom to remember for instruction: an essential first instructional step is to provide an experience of meaning in language development. The importance of using realia in language development cannot be overstated. Realia provides meaningful experiences. This was discussed in the previous chapter; however, realia must continue to be used with ELLs across levels of proficiency. At those times when you are not able to march the class out to a plant nursery at the drop of a hat, use visuals and models. Internet images are readily accessible and can approximate the meaningful experience.

Conversely, it is a common error to see teachers using word cards as a first option at this stage. Word cards are useful once students know the words but not before. Someone could have repeatedly shown me a word card with *viveros* written on it, and it would have made no difference, just as I had seen the sign for *viveros* multiple times around town without understanding what it meant. Someone could have taught me the correct pronunciation—BEE-bear-ose—but it would not have been meaningful. Until I had the experience of seeing a plant nursery, the word remained meaningless. Let me emphasize that word cards are not inherently wrong; they just are not an efficient and meaningful first option for instruction. Remember the following axiom: Meaningful experience first,

Figure 5.2 Helpful Strategies and Unhelpful Practices for Early Intermediate ELLs

Helpful Strategies	Unhelpful Practices
Providing a meaningful experience and labeling it with a word card	Showing a word card without context or visuals and asking, "What do you think this means?"
Continuing to show visuals and real objects that give clues and images about the instruction	Neglecting the value of meaningful experiences with realia and visuals as a first action of instruction
Modeling conventional speech by restating what an ELL said in a grammatically correct way	Over-correcting grammatically incorrect utterances to the extent that ELLs feel tentative about speaking
Beginning lessons on any topic with meaningful vocabulary instruction	Calling for one-word choral responses to questions
Providing opportunities to develop oral fluency with language games	Neglecting writing opportunities because students struggle with spelling, grammar, and punctuation
Providing response boards for students to write answers	Accepting only error-free writing

word cards second. Provide an authentic experience, or show the real object or a picture of the object, and then attach a label with a word card.

Figure 5.2 (above) summarizes some helpful strategies and unhelpful practices for ELLs at the early intermediate level.

Recommended Strategies for Early Intermediate Language Learners Defined

In this chapter, level 2 language behaviors and instructional applications are provided. The instructional applications listed here are described in detail on the following pages.

- ◆ Continue to use all previously employed strategies, including those involving realia, visuals, and meaningful gestures.
- ◆ Use predictable books with vivid illustrations.
- ◆ Develop storyboard frames.
- ◆ Introduce students to interactive journaling.
- ◆ Create chart stories.
- ◆ Provide direct vocabulary instruction.

Continue to Use All Previously Employed Strategies, Including Those Involving Realia, Visuals, and Meaningful Gestures

This is an important reminder that all English language learners need initial support with real objects, visuals, and meaningful gestures as a first line of strategies when introducing new learning. Providing a meaningful experience of language first is a good practice for all teaching. This is a principle of Universal Design (Burgstahler & Cory, 2008). Making an accommodation for some that will benefit the whole class is good teaching.

Use Predictable Books with Vivid Illustrations

The purpose of using predictable books (Figure 5.3) is to meaningfully establish the rhythm and content of complete sentences. Predictable pattern books provide simple sentences that change only slightly in their repetition. As ELLs are read to and chant along with the repeated sentences, they begin to acquire the use of full sentences. When selecting books for ELLs, be sure to choose ones with vivid illustrations that convey the meaning of the text.

Older students probably would not feel comfortable using the above list of children's books unless they were asked to read to younger children. However,

Figure 5.3 Easy Predictable-Pattern Books

Aliki (1989). *My five senses*. New York, NY: Thomas Y. Crowell.
Astley, J. (1990). *When one cat woke up*. New York, NY: Dial.
Baer, G. (1989). *Thump, thump, rat-a-tat-tat*. New York, NY: Harper & Row.
Barton, B. (1989). *Dinosaurs, dinosaurs*. New York, NY: Thomas Y. Crowell.
Brandenberg, F. (1989). *Aunt Nina, good night*. New York, NY: Greenwillow.
Brown, M. W. (1947). *Goodnight moon*. New York, NY: Harper & Row.
Carle, E. (1969). *The very hungry caterpillar*. New York, NY: Philomel.
Emberly, E. (1974). *Klippity klop*. Boston, MA: Little, Brown.
Hutchins, P. (1982). *1 hunter*. New York, NY: Greenwillow.
Jonas, A. (1989). *Color dance*. New York, NY: Greenwillow.
Kraus, R. (1970). *Whose mouse are you?* New York, NY: MacMillan.
Martin, B. (1991). *Polar bear, polar bear*. New York, NY: Henry Holt.
Martin, B. (1983). *Brown bear, brown bear*. New York, NY: Henry Holt.
McKissack, P. (1986). *Who is coming?* Chicago, IL: Children's Press.
McKissack, P., & McKissack, F. (1988). *Constance stumbles*. Chicago, IL: Children's Press.
Peek, M. (1985). *Mary wore her red dress*. New York, NY: Clarion.
Prelutsky, J. (Ed.) (1983). *The Random House book of poetry for children*. New York, NY: Random House.
Roffey, M. (1988). *I spy at the zoo*. New York, NY: MacMillan.
West, C. (1986). *"Pardon?" said the giraffe*. New York, NY: J.B. Lippincott.
Wildsmith, B. (1965). *Brian Wildsmith's Mother Goose*. New York, NY: Franklin Watts.
Williams, S. (1992). *I went walking*. Orlando, FL: Harcourt Brace Jovanovich.

Source: Predictable-pattern books: literacy.kent.edu/Oasis/Pubs/patterns.html

another option for older ELLs is to employ jazz chants (Graham, 2000). The concept behind jazz chants is rhythmic chanting of daily conversations. Carolyn Graham, who conceived of the idea, was a jazz piano player and singer prior to becoming a teacher of English as a second language. She naturally applied her talents in music and rhythm to learning a second language. The chants are fun and range in topics from morning greetings to what to say on a date to subject area content material. The call and response style of jazz chants provides an engaging way to repetitively practice using the vernacular of daily speech in English.

Develop Storyboard Frames

Moviemakers, such as Steven Spielberg or George Lucas, know the impact of visuals. They are experts at developing and using storyboards to convey meaning. A storyboard is basically a sequence of pictures that tell a narrative. Asking students to develop storyboards has multiple functions for language acquisition. First, storyboards indicate comprehension of a story. At a glance, a teacher can see if the students understood what happened in a story. I remember hearing of a young child who was illustrating a favorite Christmas carol, "Silent Night." The teacher looked at the picture and saw the traditional elements of the song, such as the star, the manger scene, and the mother and child. Then the teacher noticed a rotund, portly fellow in a hat and asked, "Who is that?" The young child responded by saying, "That's Round John Virgin!" Clearly, the child had a language comprehension issue here that the illustration uncovered.

Storyboards have functions other than quick checks for comprehension. They can be used to extend oral language by extending the length of a personal narrative or a story. Rather than relying on a simple retelling of story events, the sequence of pictures facilitates longer oral narratives. Additionally, storyboards provide a context for inserting more-descriptive language as appropriate.

Story sequencing is another use for storyboards. Simply slice them up into individual pictures of a story, and have students reconstruct the narratives by arranging the pictures again in order of the story sequence. This can function as a fluency game. Students share their cut-up storyboards in small groups and have their classmates try to put the pictures in order to retell the story accurately. Embedded in the activity is repetitive practice in identifying complete sentences from the narrative in a social setting.

For free templates for storyboards, see Karen J. Lloyd's Storyboard Blog (karenjlloyd.com/blog/free-storyboard-template-downloads). Lloyd encourages students to do digital storytelling that is facilitated by storyboarding, giving students the opportunity to be their own Spielberg or Lucas. Making their own movies is a highly engaging endeavor that is full of meaningful language development opportunities.

Introduce Students to Interactive Journaling

Daily writing is an essential component of literacy development at all stages, and interactive journals are ideal for introducing ELLs to writing. Even at early

Figure 5.4 Steps to Simple Interactive Journal Writing

Step 1: Write an open letter to the class; include key vocabulary.
Step 2: Read and guide choral reading of the open letter.
Step 3: Highlight the key vocabulary with underlining or color coding.
Step 4: Invite students to respond to the open letter in their journals. Set a timer for this activity (five to ten minutes)—avoid dragging it on for too long.
Step 5: Respond to the journals in writing:
 Option A: Collect the journals and write a response to each student using key vocabulary.
 Option B: Have students write in a neighbor's journal. Write in selected journals with the goal of writing in every journal at least once a week.
 Option C: Invite parent volunteers to assist as you write responses to journals with the students at their desks. Take a moment to discuss what is said and how to use conventions.

stages, with their tentative approximations at letter and word formation, ELLs can begin writing. Although it is not the appropriate stage to heavily stress exact writing conventions, the conventions of grammar, spelling, and punctuation can be individually modeled with interactive journaling. Explicit instruction of conventions is much more effective once ELLs have established a higher level of writing fluency. Until ELLs reach that level, they are much better served by being invited to write freely, orally expressing their intended written approximations, and then receiving written responses from the teacher, who uses the conventional forms of the intended words and sentences.

A simple instructional sequence for interactive journal writing begins with the teacher's writing an open letter to the class on a large sheet of paper for all to see. The open letter is no more than a couple of sentences about the day's events or something special that the teacher wants to highlight. A strategic teacher will include key words that are part of the day's instruction for vocabulary development and/or spelling. The teacher guides the students in reading the open letter, highlights key vocabulary, and then conducts a choral reading of the open letter with the entire class.

Students respond to the teacher's open letter by writing in their own journals. They are encouraged to circle the words they are not sure how to spell in order to inform the teacher about the words they want to learn. Figure 5.4 (above) shows five steps for interactive journal writing.

Create Chart Stories
The primary purposes for utilizing chart stories include a way to demonstrate the natural flow from oral language to print literacy; a venue to model

conventional spelling, grammar, and punctuation; and a forum to invite and validate the students' own words and ideas in a collaborative activity. Creating a chart story, in its basic form, simply involves using a large sheet of chart paper to write a short narrative or report of information. Chart stories are used in whole- and small-group settings to model writing. The writing is often no longer than a single paragraph. Chart stories are collaborative narratives that involve sharing ideas, suggesting words to include or the order of words, and negotiating what students intended to say.

There are unlimited possibilities with chart stories. I'll discuss the basic format and suggest some adaptations to apply chart stories for multiple instructional settings.

Basic Chart Story Format

Materials Needed

- Large poster-sized sheet of paper (lined or unlined)
- Colored marking pens
- Painter's blue masking tape (it sticks to walls without removing the painted surface)
- A classroom set of small whiteboard tablets as response boards, whiteboard markers and erasers

Procedures

1. Begin with a theme or an idea to write about. It could be something related to the day's learning, a special event, or a new topic to explore that a student suggests.
2. The teacher initiates a starter sentence: What do we know about _____ ? Have you ever heard of _____ ? Did you know that _____ ? Once upon a time, _____ . _____ is fascinating. Yesterday we saw _____ .
3. Ask students to talk with one another first about the topic. Invite them to share at least one idea with a seat partner.
4. Invite students to contribute to the chart story by sharing a complete sentence to be written on the chart paper. Insist on complete sentences to encourage language development.
5. Act as the scribe, and write the sentences on the chart paper.
6. Write new or key vocabulary in a different color to highlight the words.
7. Use a color to mark and model conventional use of punctuation.
8. Pause occasionally to ask students to write the spellings of suggested words on their response boards.
9. Pause occasionally to ask students for another way to say what they mean. Ask students, "Does this say what we want here?" This negotiation of meaning models what an author does while writing.

Some adaptations of the basic chart story follow:

♦ Conduct a collaborative interview of a guest or selected student. Write the answers to the interview questions on a chart.

♦ Use the initial chart as a way to model how to revise a paragraph. Discuss the order and flow of the sentences. Slice up the chart into individual sentences and manipulate the order for a more logical flow of ideas. Ask if anything is missing and needs to be added. Glue the rearranged sentences onto another sheet of chart paper.

♦ For informational texts, use the chart story idea to model a report of findings or a sequence of steps to solve a problem.

Provide Direct Vocabulary Instruction

For an ELL, almost all learning includes new vocabulary. A new story to read, an expansion of writing, a new concept in science, a skill in math, or even a new exercise in P.E. all involve the acquisition of new vocabulary. Key vocabulary holds the general meaning of instruction together. Therefore, direct instruction of key vocabulary at the outset of a lesson is unquestionably required. Failure to teach new vocabulary at the beginning of a lesson predictably results in confusion and loss of learning time because of repeated instruction.

As stated earlier, vocabulary is best taught with the use of realia, visuals, and meaningful gestures as a first option. Exploring an object, showing an image, or demonstrating an action carries layers of meaning that an abstract word card and definition cannot. Follow up concrete experiences with words via realia, visuals, and gestures with word cards and definitions as a second option.

Even when teachers do not have a large store of materials to make words come alive, several activities can help develop meaning. Here are few suggestions:

♦ Use a document projector, such as an Elmo, to show the meanings of words from illustrations in books.

♦ Tap Google Images as a ready resource of pictures for any word.

♦ As part of their regular homework, ask students to bring objects or pictures to class that convey the meaning of key vocabulary words.

♦ Ask students to illustrate key words for you. Display their colorful drawings next to key vocabulary on posters around the room.

♦ As part of instruction, have students make posters about important words including definitions, examples of sentences that convey appropriate usage, and illustrations of how and where the words appear in the world.

To illustrate the importance of a single key word, let me tell you about a friend who attended a lecture by a noted German philosopher. My friend had a graduate degree in philosophy. He was familiar with the lecturer's writings. However, although the lecture was delivered in English, the central idea of the lecture hung on a particular word that was not readily understandable when pronounced in a thick German accent. What my friend heard was an incomprehensible expression: *wackwoom*. The philosopher discussed a "*wackwoom* in contemporary society." Needless to say, my friend left the lecture befuddled. At the post-lecture reception, his friends and colleagues were buzzing about the brilliant lecture that he had not understood. So he got the courage to ask his colleagues what in the world *wackwoom* meant. To his embarrassment, and to the delight of his laughing colleagues, they said, "It wasn't *wackwoom*; it was *vacuum*—that there was a *vacuum* in contemporary society." Needless to say, some direct instruction of terminology prior to the lecture would have made the entire lecture fully understandable. But when one key word was incomprehensible, the meaning of the lecture was lost. The same can happen during daily classroom instruction when teachers neglect to directly and intentionally teach key vocabulary prior to a lesson.

Common Core State Standards for Listening and Speaking and Early Intermediate English Language Learners

This section provides specific examples of how to apply the appropriate strategies for early intermediate stage ELLs within the following grade ranges: K–2 (Figure 5.5), 3–5 (Figure 5.9), 6–8 (Figure 5.11), and 9–12 (Figure 5.14). Although the suggested strategies are applicable across grade levels, they will look different within grade ranges. The following examples at each grade range will demonstrate the unique features of instruction and accommodation using the suggested strategies. Additionally, the following section is intended to be exemplary rather than comprehensive.

Note to Readers: If you are a middle-school or high-school teacher, you may wish to skip ahead to your grade range at this point.

Figure 5.5 Common Core State Standards for Listening and Speaking: K–2

Kindergarten	1. Participate in collaborative conversations with diverse partners about *kindergarten topics and texts* with peers and adults in small and larger groups. a) Follow agreed-upon rules for discussions (e.g., listening to others and taking turns speaking about the topics and texts under discussion). b) Continue a conversation through multiple exchanges. 2. Confirm understanding of a text read aloud or information presented orally or through other media by asking and answering questions about key details and requesting clarification if something is not understood. **a) Understand and follow one- and two-step oral directions.** 3. Ask and answer questions in order to seek help, get information, or clarify something that is not understood.
Grade 1	1. Participate in collaborative conversations with diverse partners about *grade 1 topics and texts* with peers and adults in small and larger groups. a) Follow agreed-upon rules for

	discussions (e.g., listening to others with care, speaking one at a time about the topics and texts under discussion). b) Build on others' talk in conversations by responding to the comments of others through multiple exchanges. c) Ask questions to clear up any confusion about the topics and texts under discussion. 2. Ask and answer questions about key details in a text read aloud or information presented orally or through other media. **a) Give, restate, and follow simple two-step directions.** 3. Ask and answer questions about what a speaker says in order to gather additional information or clarify something that is not understood.
Grade 2	1. Participate in collaborative conversations with diverse partners about *grade 2 topics and texts* with peers and adults in small and larger groups. a) Follow agreed-upon rules for discussions (e.g., gaining the floor in respectful ways, listening to others with care, speaking one at a time about the topics and texts under discussion). b) Build on others' talk in conversations by linking their comments to the remarks of others. c) Ask for clarification and further explanation as needed about the topics and texts under discussion. 2. Recount or describe key ideas or details from a text read aloud or information presented orally or through other media. **a) Give and follow three- and four-step oral directions.** 3. Ask and answer questions about what a speaker says in order to clarify comprehension, gather additional information, or deepen understanding of a topic or issue.

Strategies for Comprehension and Collaboration, Grades K–2

Use a Question Cube in Small-Group Settings

A question cube is simply a small box with a question tacked to each of its six sides. A student tosses the cube to someone else in the class. The other student catches the cube, and the class discusses the question on the top side. Early intermediate stage ELLs are able to respond to open-ended questions with brief narratives or explanations, so this activity is quite appropriate for their language level. With younger children, the teacher may need to read the question for students to discuss in their groups. More-proficient students can read it to one another. Figure 5.6 (page 74) shows six questions you can use on the cube.

Instead of a question cube, some teachers simply tape questions to a beach ball and toss that around to stimulate discussion. Consider developing a bank of questions that can be substituted in and out of the discussion.

Figure 5.6 Six Questions to Use

1. What were you thinking as you listened to the story?
2. What did you picture in your mind?
3. What was your favorite part of the story? Why?
4. Who was the most interesting character? Describe him or her.
5. What would you do if you were in the story?
6. How would you change the story if you were there?

Have Students Make Their Own Question Cubes

♦ Ask students to include illustrated answers to the questions for their cubes. Ask them to draw an answer to each question and glue the drawings under the appropriate question on the cube. They then use the cubes as advanced organizers to share their thinking about the story with a partner or small group.
♦ Use the pattern in Figure 5.7 (below) to make six-sided cubes. Attach questions and student-illustrated answers to cubes prior to folding and attaching the sides.

Figure 5.7 Cube Pattern

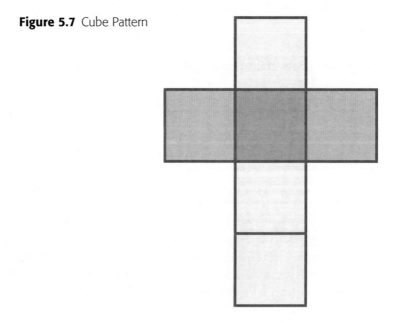

Figure 5.8 Sample Clarification Questions

Clarification Questions to Display
What did you mean when you said _____ ?
Could you repeat what you just said about _____ ?
When did this happen?
Where did this happen?
What was the most important idea? Why?
How did you do that?
What was that word _____ ? How is it spelled?

Display a Question Bank

Maintain a bulletin board with this header: What Do I Say When I Don't Understand? Include a variety of model questions that call for clarification and understanding (see Figure 5.8, above). The questions should not be a fixed set that does not change over the course of the school term. Encourage students to add to the list and/or insert new questions periodically. Use the updates as instructional moments to review questioning strategies and ways to make in-depth inquiry. The line of questions could be tailored to particular topics, such as math, history, or science.

Figure 5.9 Common Core State Standards for Listening and Speaking: Grades 3–5

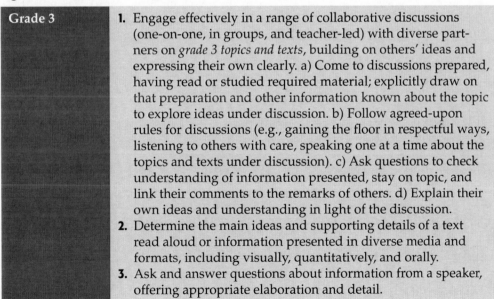

| Grade 3 | 1. Engage effectively in a range of collaborative discussions (one-on-one, in groups, and teacher-led) with diverse partners on *grade 3 topics and texts*, building on others' ideas and expressing their own clearly. a) Come to discussions prepared, having read or studied required material; explicitly draw on that preparation and other information known about the topic to explore ideas under discussion. b) Follow agreed-upon rules for discussions (e.g., gaining the floor in respectful ways, listening to others with care, speaking one at a time about the topics and texts under discussion). c) Ask questions to check understanding of information presented, stay on topic, and link their comments to the remarks of others. d) Explain their own ideas and understanding in light of the discussion.
2. Determine the main ideas and supporting details of a text read aloud or information presented in diverse media and formats, including visually, quantitatively, and orally.
3. Ask and answer questions about information from a speaker, offering appropriate elaboration and detail. |

Grade 4	1. Engage effectively in a range of collaborative discussions (one-on-one, in groups, and teacher-led) with diverse partners on *grade 4 topics and texts*, building on others' ideas and expressing their own clearly. a) Come to discussions prepared, having read or studied required material; explicitly draw on that preparation and other information known about the topic to explore ideas under discussion. b) Follow agreed-upon rules for discussions and carry out assigned roles. c) Pose and respond to specific questions to clarify or follow up on information, and make comments that contribute to the discussion and link to the remarks of others. d) Review the key ideas expressed and explain their own ideas and understanding in light of the discussion. 2. Paraphrase portions of a text read aloud or information presented in diverse media and formats, including visually, quantitatively, and orally. 3. Identify the reasons and evidence a speaker **or media source** provides to support particular points.
Grade 5	1. Engage effectively in a range of collaborative discussions (one-on-one, in groups, and teacher-led) with diverse partners on *grade 5 topics and texts*, building on others' ideas and expressing their own clearly. a) Come to discussions prepared, having read or studied required material; explicitly draw on that preparation and other information known about the topic to explore ideas under discussion. b) Follow agreed-upon rules for discussions and carry out assigned roles. c) Pose and respond to specific questions by making comments that contribute to the discussion and elaborate on the remarks of others. d) Review the key ideas expressed and draw conclusions in light of information and knowledge gained from the discussions. 2. Summarize a written text read aloud or information presented in diverse media and formats, including visually, quantitatively, and orally. 3. Summarize the points a speaker **or media source** makes and explain how each claim is supported by reasons and evidence, **and identify and analyze any logical fallacies.**

Strategies for Comprehension and Collaboration, Grades 3–5

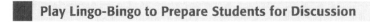 **Play Lingo-Bingo to Prepare Students for Discussion**

Discussions about a given topic are often stifled because the students are not fluent in the key terms needed for discussion. Lingo-Bingo is a socially interactive game to review and practice usage of key terminology prior to discussion. The game works like this: give each student a Lingo-Bingo sheet (see sample in

Figure 5.10, below), and ask students to mingle through the group and find a person to accurately define each term. The student who defines a term correctly signs his or her name after the word. The objective is to get a signature for each term without repeating signatures. The first person to get every term signed off yells out "Lingo-Bingo!"

Materials Needed
♦   A sheet of paper with the key terms defined. This could also be a single poster-sized paper that displays the key terms with definitions. Prior to the start of the game, remove the definitions from view.
♦   Half-sheets of paper with nine spaces and a key term written in each space, one half-sheet for each student. Students collect a signature below each term on the line marked with an X. Not allowing duplicate signatures ensures maximum interaction. A sample is shown below. The key terms in the sample are related to weather. Your topic will be different. To save time, you may ask students to write selected terms on the half-sheets on their own.

Procedures
♦   Begin with a five-minute review of the key terms and their definitions.
♦   Students start mingling, looking for a person who knows a key term and can accurately define it. That person signs the student's Lingo Bingo sheet under the term.
♦   Students keep mingling and try to obtain a different signature on the Lingo-Bingo sheet for each correctly defined term.

Figure 5.10 Sample Lingo-Bingo Vocabulary Playing Sheet
LINGO-BINGO

Temperature	Adaptation	Climate zone
X _____	X _____	X _____
Tropical	Humidity	Air pressure
X _____	X _____	X _____
Barometer	Cloud burst	Condensation
X _____	X _____	X _____

Source: Created by the author.

- ◆ Repeat signatures are not allowed; that increases the number of interactions each student must make.
- ◆ When a student has collected a signature for each term, he or she shouts "Lingo-Bingo."
- ◆ Allow five minutes for the mingling to obtain signatures.
- ◆ When all participants have reviewed and fluently used the key terminology, a more fruitful discussion of the topic can begin to take place. Even ELLs at the lowest levels can participate in this activity because they only need to ask others to tell the definitions. If low-level ELLs can define only one or two words, those are the words they may sign off on. Their job is to collect signatures from fellow students who can tell them what the words mean.

Students Role-Play Dialogue from a Story or About an Important Concept

This section of the standards calls for identifying main ideas, paraphrasing, and summarizing. An engaging way to ask students to think in those ways is to have them create a role-play scenario. Prior to creating the role-play, invite a discussion of the main points of the text. Note the main idea(s) on the board as a reference point for all students. If the text is narrative, then two or more students can re-create the characters' dialogue in their own words. Encourage students to structure the dialogue around the main points of the story that are identified on the board. If the text is informational, the students can portray two scientists or historians who are arguing for or against the main points of the concept being discussed.

Class Interviews a Fictional Character or Guest Speaker

To address the requirements of this set of standards to ask questions and analyze the answers, have students interview a fictional or historical character in a news conference format. Invite a student, or even a parent or special guest, to come to class dressed up as the interviewee. Establish the following ground rules:

- ◆ Students take turns asking questions. Alternate boys and girls for gender equity.
- ◆ The interviewee may say, "Pass" or "I don't know" in response to any question.
- ◆ Students may question sources for answers by asking questions such as "How did you learn that?" "Where did that information come from?" "Where can I find more information about that idea?"
- ◆ Using complete sentences, the person asking a question must paraphrase, or summarize, the interviewee's answer for the other students. The teacher can stand to the side and write the paraphrase or summary on a large sheet of paper.

◆ At the end of the interview, the students write summaries of the main points. This can be a homework assignment or a small-group, in-class assignment.

Figure 5.11 Common Core State Standards for Listening and Speaking: Grades 6–8

Grade 6	1. Engage effectively in a range of collaborative discussions (one-on-one, in groups, and teacher-led) with diverse partners on *grade 6 topics, texts, and issues,* building on others' ideas and expressing their own clearly. a) Come to discussions prepared, having read or studied required material; explicitly draw on that preparation by referring to evidence on the topic, text, or issue to probe and reflect on ideas under discussion. b) Follow rules for collegial discussions, set specific goals and deadlines, and define individual roles as needed. c) Pose and respond to specific questions with elaboration and detail by making comments that contribute to the topic, text, or issue under discussion. d) Review the key ideas expressed and demonstrate understanding of multiple perspectives through reflection and paraphrasing. 2. Interpret information presented in diverse media and formats (e.g., visually, quantitatively, orally) and explain how it contributes to a topic, text, or issue under study. 3. Delineate a speaker's argument and specific claims, distinguishing claims that are supported by reasons and evidence from claims that are not.
Grade 7	1. Engage effectively in a range of collaborative discussions (one-on-one, in groups, and teacher-led) with diverse partners on *grade 7 topics, texts, and issues,* building on others' ideas and expressing their own clearly. a) Come to discussions prepared, having read or researched material under study; explicitly draw on that preparation by referring to evidence on the topic, text, or issue to probe and reflect on ideas under discussion. b) Follow rules for collegial discussions, track progress toward specific goals and deadlines, and define individual roles as needed. c) Pose questions that elicit elaboration and respond to others' questions and comments with relevant observations and ideas that bring the discussion back on topic as needed. d) Acknowledge new information expressed by others and, when warranted, modify their own views. 2. Analyze the main ideas and supporting details presented in diverse media and formats (e.g., visually, quantitatively, orally) and explain how the ideas clarify a topic, text, or issue under study. 3. Delineate a speaker's argument and specific claims, **and attitude toward the subject,** evaluating the soundness of the reasoning and the relevance and sufficiency of the evidence.

Grade 8	1. Engage effectively in a range of collaborative discussions (one-on-one, in groups, and teacher-led) with diverse partners on *grade 8 topics, texts, and issues,* building on others' ideas and expressing their own clearly. a) Come to discussions prepared, having read or researched material under study; explicitly draw on that preparation by referring to evidence on the topic, text, or issue to probe and reflect on ideas under discussion. b) Follow rules for collegial discussions and decision-making, track progress toward specific goals and deadlines, and define individual roles as needed. c) Pose questions that connect the ideas of several speakers and respond to others' questions and comments with relevant evidence, observations, and ideas. d) Acknowledge new information expressed by others, and, when warranted, qualify or justify their own views in light of the evidence presented. 2. Analyze the purpose of information presented in diverse media and formats (e.g., visually, quantitatively, orally) and evaluate the motives (e.g., social, commercial, political) behind its presentation. 3. Delineate a speaker's argument and specific claims, evaluating the soundness of the reasoning and relevance and sufficiency of the evidence and identifying when irrelevant evidence is introduced.

Strategies for Comprehension and Collaboration, Grades 6–8

 Use an Advanced Organizer to Facilitate Discussion and Active Learning

One of the best ways to address the preceding standards for ELLs at the early intermediate stage of proficiency is to help prepare them for discussion and participation in active learning with advanced organizers. Advanced organizers are designed in a variety of ways. Simply conduct an Internet search of advanced organizers to see the multiple forms available. For the purposes of facilitating an organized discussion and active learning task, I recommend a three-part advanced organizer that includes the following components: (1) essential content, (2) task overview, and (3) critical reflection. A sample is shown in Figure 5.12 (page 81). Here are the advanced organizer components in detail:

◆ *Essential content:* This part of the advanced organizer includes a brief statement of an overview of the learning that will be explored and key vocabulary listed and defined. It also includes the sources for essential content, such as references to texts or websites that inform the learning.

Figure 5.12 Sample of an Advanced Organizer

Advanced Organizer

Essential Content
Academic learning goal: (to be populated by the teacher)
Key vocabulary: (listed and defined)
Sources and resources:
Something I know about this topic:

Task Overview
What to do:
Materials list:
Questions to consider:
Description of the final product:

Critical Reflection
What was your role?
What did you do?
What did you, or your group, do well?
What needs to improve?
What did you learn?

◆ *Task overview:* This part outlines a particular task for individuals or a small group to complete. The section includes an academic learning goal, or objective, for the task; a list of required materials to complete the task; a set of directions and questions to address; and a description of the final product, if required.
◆ *Critical reflection:* In this section, the individual or group responds to questions that evaluate the quality of the process and the product of the learning activity.

Evaluate Information from Diverse Media Sources

Figure 5.13 (page 82) is a simple tool that can facilitate analyzing information from a guest lecture, an opinion piece from a newspaper, a letter to the editor, or a media source. The tool examines a text from a pro vs. con perspective. The first questions look at the topic itself and what information is missing. The second questions ask the student to state the stance of the information and to articulate the opposition. The final questions look at the sources, or lack thereof, for the information being presented.

The tool is helpful for early intermediate ELLs because it helps them clearly organize their thoughts with a few words or phrases so they can take sides in a

Figure 5.13 Sample Information Analysis Student Work Sheet

Information Analysis

Pro	Con
What topics are being covered?	What topics are being ignored?
Describe what is being advocated:	Describe what is being opposed:
What are the sources (if any)?	What sources are not included?

Source: Adapted from Douglas Gould and Company, "Writing a Media Analysis," (2004)

discussion. I recommend that this information analysis tool be used in pairs or in small groups followed by a discussion of opposing points of view.

Figure 5.14 Common Core State Standards for Listening and Speaking: Grades 9–12

Note: Readers will see that the following standards for high-school students are very similar from grade to grade with only minor differences. Further, the standards are multifaceted and complex. An English language learner at level 2, the early intermediate stage, cannot realistically be expected to participate at the same level as a native speaker; however, the group can be asked to comply with the standards by establishing rules of conduct that invite the participation of ELLs. The group can utilize media sources to make discussion and interaction more comprehensible. The discussion rubric presented in chapter 4 can be applied across all language levels.

Grades 9–10	
	1. Initiate and participate effectively in a range of collaborative discussions (one-on-one, in groups, and teacher-led) with diverse partners on *grades 9–10 topics, texts, and issues,* building on others' ideas and expressing their own clearly and persuasively. a) Come to discussions prepared, having read and researched material under study; explicitly draw on that preparation by referring to evidence from texts and other research on the topic or issue to stimulate a thoughtful, well-reasoned exchange of ideas. b) Work with peers to set rules for collegial discussions and decision-making (e.g., informal consensus, taking votes on key issues, presentation

of alternate views), clear goals and deadlines, and individual roles as needed. c) Propel conversations by posing and responding to questions that relate the current discussion to broader themes or larger ideas; actively incorporate others into the discussion; and clarify, verify, or challenge ideas and conclusions. d) Respond thoughtfully to diverse perspectives, summarize points of agreement and disagreement, and, when warranted, qualify or justify their own views and understanding and make new connections in light of the evidence and reasoning presented.

2. Integrate multiple sources of information presented in diverse media or formats (e.g., visually, quantitatively, orally) evaluating the credibility and accuracy of each source.

3. Evaluate a speaker's point of view, reasoning, and use of evidence and rhetoric, identifying any fallacious reasoning or exaggerated or distorted evidence.

Grades 11–12	1. Initiate and participate effectively in a range of collaborative discussions (one-on-one, in groups, and teacher-led) with diverse partners on *grades 11–12 topics, texts, and issues*, building on others' ideas and expressing their own clearly and persuasively. a) Come to discussions prepared, having read and researched material under study; explicitly draw on that preparation by referring to evidence from texts and other research on the topic or issue to stimulate a thoughtful, well-reasoned exchange of ideas. b) Work with peers to promote civil, democratic discussions and decision-making, set clear goals and deadlines, and establish individual roles as needed. c) Propel conversations by posing and responding to questions that probe reasoning and evidence; ensure a hearing for a full range of positions on a topic or issue; clarify, verify, or challenge ideas and conclusions; and promote divergent and creative perspectives. d) Respond thoughtfully to diverse perspectives; synthesize comments, claims, and evidence made on all sides of an issue; resolve contradictions when possible; and determine what additional information or research is required to deepen the investigation or complete the task.
	2. Integrate multiple sources of information presented in diverse formats and media (e.g., visually, quantitatively, orally) in order to make informed decisions and solve problems, evaluating the credibility and accuracy of each source and noting any discrepancies among the data.
	3. Evaluate a speaker's point of view, reasoning, and use of evidence and rhetoric, assessing the stance, premises, links among ideas, word choice, points of emphasis, and tone used.

Strategies for Comprehension and Collaboration, Grades 9–12

Use Jigsaw Techniques

Jigsaw techniques (Slavin, 2011) are used to help a group of participants actively review a text and co-teach one another the content. Although jigsaw techniques were initiated at the elementary grades, they are useful in high-school and adult-learning settings as well. In a study of the effectiveness of jigsaw classrooms, Moskowitz et al. (1983) found that the techniques were highly correlated with increased classroom participation and attendance. The group practice of reliance on one another with specific roles fostered higher levels of student engagement and responsibility for the learning. The technique involves organizing a text into segments, assigning small groups to become experts on their particular segment of the text, and then having the expert participants teach students who were assigned other segments. With the added factor of English language learners being active participants, I recommend a slight adaptation: use expert pairs in the small groups so that an ELL is not solely responsible for teaching the rest of the group.

Procedures
♦ Select a text for the class to read and discuss.
♦ Decide whether to organize the text into four or six segments. This will determine the length of the passage and size of the expert groups. Consider the number of students in your class (example: $36 \div 4 = 8$/expert group, or $36 \div 6 = 6$/expert group).
♦ Label the segments of text A, B, C, D, E, F, depending on the number of segments.
♦ Establish the expert groups. Expert group A is assigned section A of the text, expert group B is assigned section B of the text, and so forth.
♦ Ask students to form partnerships within expert groups. If numbers allow, partner English language learners with native speakers. Another option is to partner higher level ELLs with lower level ELLs. Therefore within an expert group of eight participants, there would be four pairs of expert partners; and within an expert group of six participants, there would be three pairs of expert partners.
♦ Number each pair within an expert group; for example, expert group A has pairs 1, 2, 3, and so forth.
♦ When the groupings are set, ask each group to read its assigned segment of the text, aloud if need be. Discuss the meaning of the text so that all are clear on what it says.
♦ Ask the expert groups to write down the important ideas and to make sure that participants can define and explain key terms to one another.
♦ Once the expert groups are ready to teach others about their assigned version of the text, reorganize the groupings into teaching groups that combine representative expert pairs for each segment of the text.

♦ Ask the expert pairs to teach their colleagues about the text, using their outlines of the main ideas and knowledge of key vocabulary. Encourage the development and usage of visual representations of the concepts and vocabulary to make the instruction more engaging.

Let me reiterate that this is where pairing an ELL with a native speaker or higher-level ELL can facilitate the learning. The two can decide which section to teach; that allows individuals to teach to their strengths. In some settings, such as urban classrooms, the ratio of low level ELLs to native speakers is much higher. Some classrooms have no high level ELLs or native speakers. Nevertheless, the jigsaw technique allows ELLs to read and rehearse the concepts and vocabulary in a text so that they can teach colleagues. The effort involves listening, speaking, reading, writing, and, at times, visually representing ideas. All of these skills are essential for active group participation.

Use Problem-Solving Pods for Quantitative Material

Standard 2 calls for integrating multiple sources of information in problem-solving settings with a range of material, including quantitative. The problem-solving pod is a variation of the jigsaw technique with a simpler grouping arrangement. The teacher also takes a more active role in direct instruction. I refer to the groupings as pods because they are groups of three students, each with an assigned responsibility: numbers and calculations, drawing and graphics, and vocabulary and writing.

Materials
♦ Class set of large sheets of graph paper
♦ Pencils
♦ Erasers
♦ Colored pencils
♦ Marking pens
♦ Drawing tools, such as protractor and compasses as needed

Procedures
♦ Organize the class into pods of three students each.
♦ Assign the following responsibilities to students: student 1—numbers and calculations; student 2—drawing and graphics; student 3—vocabulary and writing.
♦ Give the class a problem to solve that requires the use of complex numbers, visual representation, and written expression.
♦ Read the problem in groups, and ask students to identify the objective and questions and to highlight key vocabulary.
♦ Call together only the students who are in charge of numbers and calculations. Discuss with them the features of the problem. Identify the

significant numbers. Discuss the various functions needed to solve the problem. Then send them back to teach their own pods.

◆ Call together the students who are in charge of drawing and graphics. Discuss the ways that the problem could be visually represented and how best to draw or represent the problem graphically. Consider multiple ways, and let the students decide what way they prefer.

◆ Call together the students who are in charge of vocabulary and writing. Make sure that they have identified each key term, what it means, and how it is spelled. Briefly outline ways to write about a solution and how to use academic language with transition words, such as proper verb tense for reporting information and when to use *therefore, in other words*, and transitional words and phrases. In some cases, the discussion would include identifying appropriate sources and citing source material.

◆ Ask each pod to use large graph paper to record numbers and calculations, drawings, and a written statement of the problem and its solution.

◆ At the end of the period, or the next day, have the problem-solving pods present their work to the rest of the class.

◆ Discuss each aspect of the presentations and decide which group(s) did the best job of accurately solving the problem and presenting the solution with numbers, graphics, and written language. See the next section for a peer rating scale.

Use a Peer Rating Scale to Evaluate Pod Presentations

The rating-scale tool in Figure 5.15 (page 87) was specifically designed to address the quality of the presentations and problem solving from the previous activity with problem-solving pods. The purpose of a rating scale is to quickly generate numeric data on a 10-point scale about the favorability of each aspect of the presentation of problem solving. I used the terms *unfavorable* and *favorable* for several reasons. The rating is an opinion, not a grade. I left it open-ended with a comment section so that peers could elaborate on what they liked or did not like about either the presentation or the quality of the solution. Sometimes the least favorable presentation has the most accurate solution, and sometimes the nicest presentation is inaccurate or flawed.

Other features of the scale include the ease of recording opinions as a group or by individuals. The numbers are easy to sum and average. The comment sections were designed to be brief and not onerous for an ELL to complete. In some cases, an anonymous rating is preferred to foster honesty or to reduce social tensions in a group; therefore, the final section about recording the raters' names is optional. Use the rating scale as a means to foster discussion about what constitutes a quality presentation of problem solving. The intention is to make clear how to improve speaking to a group, representing one's work, and identifying the best solution to a problem.

Figure 5.15 Sample Problem Solving Peer Rating Scale

Problem Solving Peer Rating Scale

Name of the group being evaluated:

Total Score: _____
Average Score: _____

Directions: Record the name of the group being evaluated. Circle the number on each scale that rates the favorability of the presentation and solution of the problem. Calculate and record the total and the average score.

Numbers and Calculations

Unfavorable _____ Favorable
    1   2   3   4   5   6   7   8   9   10
Comments:

Drawings and Graphics

Unfavorable _____ Favorable
    1   2   3   4   5   6   7   8   9   10
Comments:

Vocabulary and Writing

Unfavorable _____ Favorable
    1   2   3   4   5   6   7   8   9   10
Comments:

Raters' Names *(optional):*

6

Level 3: The Intermediate Stage and Common Core Listening and Speaking

After a year, or more, of second-language development, English language learners predictably move into level 3, the intermediate stage of proficiency. This stage is characterized by an expanded use of oral language and a more fluent use of written language. At this stage, the ELL can be much more self-expressive and is able to read slightly more-complex material. For the first two stages, instruction regarding text complexity might not have been appropriate, but teaching text complexity is more viable at this stage provided ELLs receive dedicated linguistic and instructional support, commonly known as *scaffolding* (Bruner, 1972).

The potential problem at this stage is that ELLs hit a plateau and risk remaining there instead of eventually progressing to higher levels of proficiency. Below, I discuss a systematic approach to addressing long-term English (LTEs) language learners. I also highlight how using cognates and etymologies are valuable ways to develop literacy at this stage. As with the previous two chapters, instructional strategies and activities for intermediate stage ELLs align with the Common Core State Standards for Listening and Speaking according to the following grade level ranges: K–2, 3–5, 6–8, and 9–12.

Long-Term English Language Learners (LTEs)

Intermediate stage proficiency is highly functional for a wide range of tasks, such as communicating needs, deciphering text, retelling events, and writing brief forms of communication. Students at this stage, however, need systemic support in developing oral and written fluency across academic disciplines in order to succeed in school and society. There is a problem for students at this stage. A systemic flaw in schools today is to make the false assumption that ELLs are "fluent enough" at this stage to function as well as other classmates without systemic linguistic and content area related instructional supports from the entire community. Students who remain at this stage struggle with content area material and the rigor of schoolwork in general. Unfortunately, too many ELLs remain at this plateau and become classified as LTEs (Olsen, 2010).

This stage in particular is a pivotal time to ensure that there are multiple resources to make the content comprehensible and to provide help with homework, family literacy programs, equal access to materials, and individual follow-up with each ELL. Superintendents and school administrators are vital in creating a culture of literacy across subject areas and throughout school districts. In short, the entire educational community has a responsibility to develop a systemic approach to support that begins with the classroom, is consistent throughout a school, is offered after school, and is supported at home. It is no longer viable to simply make the classroom teacher the only person accountable for students' success.

One thing that classroom teachers can do to begin the process of developing a systemic approach to meeting the needs of LTEs is begin to organize at the elementary level according to grade level groups and at the secondary level according to subject area groups. Organizing a group requires setting a specific task for its members. At least initially, I would suggest that grade level and subject area groups form around a book study. Select a book related to English language development across the curriculum. With shared knowledge gained from studying a quality book, teachers will have the resources at the ready to approach their school administrators with systemic solutions to addressing the needs of LTEs. Guidelines for forming a book study group are available at the Eye On Education website: www.routledge.com.

School administrators have a unique responsibility to be proactive in setting up school-wide systems that involve the community in developing literacy for all students. For example, one school administrator initiated a parent literacy center that taught parents how to help their children with writing skills. In addition to teaching the parents, the center became a place where teachers could send struggling writers for one-on-one help with trained parents, under the guidance of an educational professional. Furthermore, the center was fully equipped with writing tools, reference resources, and writing materials to help the parents work with the students. When the parents did not know what to do, the educational professional used the moment for instruction to parents whose kids needed help. This model had a double benefit of helping students and training parents to help their kids. It was highly cost effective and engaged the community in helping parents and kids help one another.

The parent literacy center was only one model for creating a systemic approach to helping LTEs so that they did not remain at a plateau. The possibilities are limited only by the imagination. For example, one of my master's degree students, a kindergarten teacher, saw the need for community support for literacy development while at the local public library. She noticed that many of the families of her students were going to the library after school and on weekends, but there were no programs to help families with reading. She met with her principal to discuss what to do, and the two of them set up a meeting with the city's mayor and head librarian. In short, together they wrote a grant to create a coordinated library/school family literacy program that provided reading assistance and story times after school and on weekends. According to Shin and Krashen (2007), the number of books available to English language learners as compared with their English-speaking classmates is dramatically less. They recommend using public libraries as the most cost-effective way to get books into the hands of ELLs.

Along those same lines, an almost free way to involve the community in developing literacy is to coordinate a parents' field trip to the local public library. In my experience, librarians are delighted to present the various programs that they offer. In addition, as part of the field trip, parents are able to sign up for library cards for themselves and their children. I once took a group of Khmer-speaking Cambodian parents on a walking field trip to the local library. Many had never entered the library before, thinking erroneously that it operated more like a bookstore than a public service. When we left that morning, more than 30 parents had new library cards and new knowledge about a public service that would help develop their children's literacy and enrich their own lives.

At the secondary level, one of the most significant systemic changes that school administrators can foster is to provide professional development that emphasizes that all teachers are responsible for the literacy development of their students within every subject area. Subject matter competence must include learning and using the language of the discipline. Math, science, and, yes, even P.E. teachers must approach their subjects with this dual notion of teaching content and discipline-specific language. In this approach, math teachers require their students to write about problems and solutions using appropriate language conventions and terminology. Science teachers demonstrate how to make sense of informational texts and how to write reports of experiments using the appropriate discourse style with past tense verbs and passive voice. P.E. teachers, in addition to teaching the skills and rules of sports, also teach the vocabulary of bones, muscles, and tendons. Let's not forget that English teachers must also expand their repertoire of instruction. They continue to teach language conventions and literary theory, but they must also creatively bring their texts to life using visuals, media, and graphic organizers and provide ample opportunities for oral presentations and discussions. Every discipline shares in the process of helping English language learners develop literacy. All teachers share the responsibility to teach the content and language of their disciplines. Every administrator ensures that programs, supports, and instructional approaches are consistently maintained system-wide and engage the community.

Figure 6.1 (below) summarizes helpful strategies and unhelpful practices for level 3 ELLs.

The Intermediate Stage English Language Learner

Identifiable language behaviors of a student at the intermediate stage are the following:

- Retells using expanded vocabulary
- Identifies main ideas and details
- Summarizes
- Makes comparisons
- Defines new vocabulary

Figure 6.1 Helpful Strategies and Unhelpful Practices

Helpful Strategies	Unhelpful Practices
Providing systemic, school-wide academic supports that involve the community	Placing the burden of language development solely on the shoulders of the classroom teacher
Practicing literacy development in all subject area disciplines	Excluding parents and family members from actively participating in children's learning
Beginning to learn new concepts with explicit and concrete vocabulary instruction	Falsely assuming that ELLs understand what they read because they can read all of the words aloud and pronounce them correctly
Continuing to show visuals and real objects that give clues and images about the instruction	Teaching with misapplied false cognates
Providing reading previews, including overviews, highlights of difficult passages, and new vocabulary	Using dictionary definitions exclusively to explain the meanings of words without providing appropriate linguistic supports
Providing a purpose for reading assigned passages	Failing to allow wait time for ELLs to think about their answers before responding
Inviting comparisons by asking, "What is this like?," "What is it not like?," and "What else is it like?"	Assigning copying of definitions from word lists
Helping students expand their sentences with alternative adjectives, richer verbs, and transitional phrases	Mocking a student's misspellings
Evaluating writing according to the content of ideas as well as writing conventions	Evaluating writing *only* according to conventions (grammar, spelling, and punctuation) and neglecting the content of the ideas
Demonstrating how to take notes and making what to write down explicit during class lectures and discussions	Requiring note-taking without modeling what to write down and how to write the notes

Retells Using Expanded Vocabulary

As stated earlier, level 3, intermediate stage, is characterized by more fluent and expanded use of language. This is one of the key differences between level 2 and level 3 ELLs. A level 2 ELL would say something such as the following: "There a car go by fast." A level 3 ELL would say, "That *blue* car go *really* fast." Although both expressions are grammatically incorrect, the level 2's expression is characterized by the bare essentials noun/verb phrase. The level 3's expression includes modifiers. The use of more-descriptive language is a particular strength to build on. This shift in language usage from limited, essential expression to using more-expanded vocabulary suggests that it is time to teach adjectives and adverbs. The teacher needs to invite new words to help students describe what is on their minds with greater detail.

Identifies Main Ideas and Details

When reading stories or informational texts, level 3 ELLs will naturally begin to talk about their reading by identifying details. It is very common for students to begin talking about their reading by talking about their favorite parts. This is an opener for dialogue about the important details of a passage. When students talk about their favorite parts, they bring in details that are meaningful to their world. Knowing what is meaningful to ELLs makes teaching easier because teachers can use familiar details to connect to other, less familiar details and bring context to the discussion naturally. Furthermore, identifying a large number of details helps build an array, or a pattern, that shows the main idea of a story or passage.

Summarizes

The ability to use expanded vocabulary and to identify important details is foundational to being able to summarize an event, a passage, or a story. In addition to identifying details is the skill of distinguishing between important and incidental details. Although ELLs will naturally begin to summarize details in brief retellings of events, they do not automatically distinguish between important and incidental details. This skill must be fostered through graphic organizers and dialogue.

Makes Comparisons

Human beings make comparisons naturally. In order to understand the world, English speakers often use phrases such as "this is like . . ." or "this is not like . . ." The linguistic action of making comparisons pushes ELLs to find new words to express their thinking. Making comparisons is the beginning point of metaphorical thinking. A teacher says, "The sun is like a big ball of fire." The students get a mental picture of what the sun is. Of course, the comparison does not do justice to the size and complexity of the sun, but it offers a workable linguistic handle to aid recall in the form of an image, a big ball of fire. Taking it a step further, the teacher asks, "What else is the sun like?" The second question pushes other words into the instruction and opens an invitation to diverse thinking.

When teachers invite comparisons by asking such questions as "What is it like?" or "What do you picture in your mind?" or "What else is it like?," they invite ELLs to express their ways of seeing and understanding the world and can incorporate that knowledge into instruction. Utilizing ELLs' perspectives taps into prior knowledge and ways of understanding things. Whether teachers recognize it or not, perceptions of the world are culturally bound. For example, if you ask someone from the midwestern United States to talk about the seasons, the person will describe four basic seasons, the clothing they wear, and activities that they do throughout the seasonal changes. But if you ask someone from the Philippines to talk about the seasons, he or she will naturally describe two seasons—the dry season and the monsoon, or rainy season, and ways seasonal changes affect life in the Philippines. Prior experiences inform entirely different perceptions of the word *season*.

Therefore, making comparisons is more than a language behavior. It is also a window into the mind of another person and his or her prior experiences and knowledge, which can be used as foundational building blocks for language development. At the intermediate stage, teachers help students develop language by assisting them in expressing their own ideas and perceptions of the world. This applies to comparing ideas about what a story character is like or not like, and it also applies to making scientific comparisons of the similarities and differences between, for example, an alligator from the Florida Keys and a caiman from Guatemala. Making comparisons demands that people access new words to enrich personal expression and metaphorical thinking.

Defines New Vocabulary

Two processes are included in this language behavior for intermediate stage ELLs. First, the act of defining words, of noting the definition of words, is a formal aspect of academic language. Prior to this stage, ELLs were acquiring words to use in simple speech; now they begin to use reference tools such as glossaries, dictionaries, and thesauri to note and record the meanings of words.

Second, this behavior implies that ELLs begin to take active roles in finding out the meanings of words for themselves. With more than 1,000,000 words in the English lexicon, it is beyond the scope of any teacher to explicitly teach all the words in the language. At this point, ELLs learn how to pursue the meanings of words more on their own.

Teachers still need to teach vocabulary explicitly and to demonstrate how to use reference tools to find the meanings of words. However, never falsely assume that when ELLs look words up in a dictionary that they understand the definition they just attempted to read. Avoid replicating the poor instructional practice of having students copy definitions from glossaries or dictionaries in the name of vocabulary development. I can't think of a quicker way to turn off students to learning about words than to assign copying definitions from word lists. There are many ways for students to learn word meanings and also develop a love of language.

Recommended Strategies for Intermediate Language Learners Defined

In this chapter, level 3 language behaviors and instructional applications are provided. The instructional applications are as follows:

- Tap experiences
- Teach study skills
- Use cognates
- Explore word origins
- Teach writing for a purpose
- Use and create media

This short list of appropriate strategies is found on the CALL assessment tool. They are not the only strategies to employ, but they correspond to the language behaviors that are unique to ELLs at this stage of language development. As you may have noted from previous chapters, there is a progression of strategies that require increasingly more complex linguistic skills at each stage. This is an additive progression that seeks to keep using the previously described strategies while adding new ones. In other words, the use of realia and visuals, though not mentioned to the same extent in this chapter, is just as applicable in the intermediate stage as in any other. Below is a more detailed discussion of how to teach using each strategy.

Tap Experiences

A primary goal for level 3 ELLs is to expand their ability to express themselves. The most efficient, cost-effective way to tap into student experiences is to ask aesthetic questions (Cox, 1994). Aesthetic questions invite students to explore their own thinking and perceptions about an experience or a topic. Conversely, questions that teachers frequently ask, such as "What were the events of the story?" or "What was the problem/solution?," call on students to reply with set answers. Aesthetic questions, on the other hand, give insight into the cultural perceptions and diverse thinking of the students. Figure 6.2 (page 96) offers some sample aesthetic questions.

So what? Why is there a need to tap into student thinking and prior experiences? From a sociocultural perspective, contemporary U.S. society is increasingly diverse. That means that students and teachers may have very few shared experiences in life. With less common ground for understanding the world, it is important for teachers to find out what students think and how they perceive what they read in order to teach for better comprehension. From an instructional perspective, teaching is much more comprehensible when the learners' cultural context is brought into the classroom.

For example, once my students and I were studying the animals of the Brazilian rain forest and the tree sloth in particular. One of the students giggled and

Figure 6.2 Sample Aesthetic Questions

Aesthetic Questions
What were you thinking?
What else are you thinking about?
What did you picture in your mind?
What was your favorite part? Why?
Put yourself in the character's place. What would you do?
How would you do this differently?
Can you think of a similar experience? What happened?

Source: Adapted from Cox (1992)

said that it had a coconut head. I could have ignored that comment as a funny comparison, but I seized the moment instead and pursued the student's line of thinking? "What else do you see?" I asked. The student said, "It has a nose like a chocolate bar." Another student chimed in with, "Its eyes are like coffee beans." Another said, "And its body is like a papaya." And another said, "Its claws are like bananas." Before I knew it, we had conceived of a metaphorical "fruit sloth."

Interestingly, each of the comparisons consistently was an item that grew in or around the rain forest (coconut, cocoa, coffee, papaya, bananas). I asked students to each bring an item to school the next day to build a "fruit sloth." We constructed the sloth according to the similes the students divined. Students then wrote short stories and poems about the sloth. They had fun with the metaphors, but they also included factual information about what they had learned, such as that sloths sleep 18 hours a day and the young cling to their mothers' backs. We finished the day with a fruit sloth feast as students read their writings about the sloth to one another.

I could have ignored the coconut head comment and asked students to write about the information found in the text exclusively; but instead, I invited their thinking into the instruction. Consider the result of asking a simple question: "What else do you see?" Students at the intermediate stage need to expand their vocabularies and expressiveness. The fruit sloth opened a rich, engaging learning experience, which invited their thinking, expanded their language, and included them as active participants in the curriculum. The official curriculum was never disregarded; it was enriched because their experiences were tapped.

Teach Study Skills

There are basically two facets to taking useful notes in class. The student needs a format to support taking clear and useful notes. On the other hand, the teacher has the responsibility to provide clearly organized information that is well outlined and visually represented.

I recommend the use of a double-entry journal for note-taking. Double-entry journal pages are a simple form of organizer with just two columns (see my

Figure 6.3 Sample Double-Entry Journal

Subject: Science

Date: April 4

Important points of information
Hammerhead sharks swim around
   tropical reefs.
Great white sharks live in deep
   water.

Reflect on your thinking
I wonder if the hammerhead and
the great white shark eat the same
things?

Draw sketches and diagrams

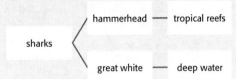

Cite pages in the text
Chapter 4, pp. 56–72

Key vocabulary
Tropical reef
Shark
Hammerhead
Great white

To-do list
Read pages 60–65: due Wednesday
Write shark report: due Friday

example in Figure 6.3, above). Generally, the left-hand column is for noting important points of information, page numbers, and key vocabulary. The right-hand column is for writing brief reflective comments, sketching drawings, and writing to-do lists. TeacherVision.fen.com offers printable templates for double-entry journals and other instructional items. However, students can simply draw a vertical line down the center of pieces of paper to make their own two-column, double-entry journal pages.

Once the note-taking format, such as the double-entry journal is established, the teacher has the responsibility to structure lectures and discussions according to that format to ensure clarity and usefulness of the notes. For instance, what is written on the board or projected on a screen should include an outline of the important points, cited pages from the text or resource material, and key vocabulary. Furthermore, structure time within lectures for students to write brief reflections about their thinking. Ask them to draw diagrams or sketches to visually represent their thinking, and give them a moment to write to-do lists with due dates included.

Modeling what to write is extremely helpful, particularly at the beginning of a school term. I highly recommend projecting a double-entry journal on a screen or posting a large sheet of two-column paper to show what notes to write. Demonstrate plausible questions to write down and possible diagrams to draw, including meaningful doodles. Write down the vocabulary words, demonstrate their meaning, and discuss their meaning. Show students how to write a brief definition. Model what should go into a to-do list, including the due date. In time, the process will become more automatic, but at the outset of a school year, it is model, model, model.

Use Cognates

Cognates are words that share a common heritage across languages. Literally, *cognate* means "of the same parentage"; linguistically, the word means "from the same language source." Cognates provide meaningful terminology that is readily accessible with a minimum of scaffolds for instruction. They are unique words that are bridges between languages. For example, I found it surprising that the word for *whale* in the Cambodian language, Khmer, is *baleen*. In English, we use the word *baleen* to describe certain whales, such as humpbacks, because they have a keratin substance, *baleen*, in their mouths instead of teeth to filter krill to eat. The language source for *baleen* is Latin, which is shared by English, French, and other Romance languages. It is shared with Khmer because Cambodia was once a colony of France. This cognate gives some insight into the dynamic nature of languages; they are not static but in constant revision because of historical and political factors.

English is considered the global language of commerce, and French is the global language of diplomacy. Therefore, thousands of words appear as cognates in languages all over the world. At the intermediate stage, ELLs increasingly learn content area literacy, such as the language of math or science, as they develop subject matter competence. Within those subject areas are a vast quantity of terms that share Latin or Greek language sources, which are parent languages to English and French. According to Cognate Linguistics.org, (www .cognates.org), more than 20,000 words in English, in the areas of math and science, are cognates with other languages. Obviously, those language sources are not as ubiquitous in Asian languages, but many of the math and science cognates are appropriated across numerous languages and become touch points of meaning for ELLs.

Cognates are like bridges between languages that foster immediate comprehension. Carlo et al. (2004) strongly advocated the use of cognates for teaching, particularly in content areas. However, a word of caution: beware of using false cognates. There are dozens of hilarious examples of misappropriated cognates, such as asking to wash hands with *sopa* (soup) instead of *jabón* (soap). I highly recommend that teachers prepare to use cognates judiciously and strategically in their lesson planning, not on the fly. Look to websites such as www.cognates .org to choose appropriate cognates for instruction. I discuss how to use etymologies as a language development strategy in the following section.

Explore Word Origins

Etymology is the study of the history of words—their origins and how their usage has changed over time. Tracing etymologies can foster knowing the stories behind the words. Knowing a word's origin helps an ELL recognize root words within other words. Etymologies also provide a deeper understanding of the words themselves. They give words, which might appear to be abstract on

Figure 6.4 Sample Etymology

Spirit (n.): mid-13c., "animating or vital principle in man and animals," from O.Fr. *espirit*, from L. *spiritus* "soul, courage, vigor, breath," related to *spirare* "to breathe," from PIE *(s)peis- "to blow" (cf. O.C.S. *pisto* "to play on the flute".)

Source: Online Etymology Dictionary, www.etymonline.com/index.php?l=a

the surface, a story or an image that contributes to greater comprehension and retention.

Reading an etymology, however, is an exercise in deciphering technical language, which is chock-full of abbreviations for languages, word examples from other languages, parts of speech, and segmented words (see sample etymology in Figure 6.4, above). An etymology is not written for an intermediate stage ELL to read for comprehension. Tracing the etymology of a word is a valuable teacher resource. I recommend tracing the etymology of words in order to tell the story of a word's origin to the class.

The etymology of the word *spirit* points to the notion of breath. It comes from the same root found in re*spir*ation, e*xpir*ation, in*spir*ation, and con*spir*acy. People and many other animals have spirit when they breathe, or re*spire*. They no longer have spirit when we e*xpire*. They give life and breath when they in*spire*. And people whisper, or plan, together when they con*spire*, or breathe together.

Knowing the etymology of *spirit* as breath gives an ELL a physical action and mental picture of the word that would otherwise be abstract and difficult to recall. Imagine utilizing Total Physical Response (Asher, 1969) to have students blow on their hands to demonstrate the root word *spirit* for re*spir*ation and huddling together and whispering to demonstrate con*spire*. The key to using etymologies is to do your homework as a teacher. It is more than looking up a word. It is exploring and tracing its meaning and story so that you can tell students the deeper meaning of the word in very concrete and memorable ways.

Teach Writing for a Purpose

Becoming a writer involves learning the skills and conventions related to print literacy. Developing the sense of being an author is just as important. To develop a sense of authorship, students need an authentic reason to write. Conversely, if students misunderstand writing as just an assignment or only a response to a prompt, it will be perceived as a chore to be done on behalf of the teacher.

There are numerous ways to foster writing for a purpose. Some suggestions are shown in Figure 6.5 (page 100). Actually, when I realized that I could have my students work on letters to parents to announce events, to request materials, or to invite participation in an activity, I not only saved myself a tremendous amount of work but also provided students with authentic ways to write.

Figure 6.5 Suggestions for Teaching Writing for a Purpose

Write
- ◆ An invitation to parents to attend a school function
- ◆ An invitation to a community leader to speak to the class
- ◆ An invitation to the principal to discuss a problem at school

- ◆ A letter of praise to a local, state, or national official
- ◆ A letter of complaint to a local, state, or national official
- ◆ A letter of recommendation on behalf of a classmate for a job or scholarship
- ◆ A letter of appreciation to a staff member at school for his or her fine work

- ◆ To a favorite author about his or her work
- ◆ To an author who is not appreciated to critique the work
- ◆ To a sports editor about a favorite team or player
- ◆ To a publisher to request a specific genre of literature

- ◆ A request to parents for specific classroom materials or food for a party
- ◆ A request to a local business for sponsorship or donations to the class

- ◆ A response to a blog posting
- ◆ A response to a posting in a threaded discussion

I would get very tired of hearing students come to class complaining about something that had happened in the school yard during a break or recess. Then someone suggested that I have students write their complaints down on paper. I set up a writing station with pencils, erasers, and half-sheets of scrap paper. As students entered the room, if they had complaints, I directed them to write down their complaints. I did not take class time to listen to oral complaints and reviewed only written complaints. This led to scheduling time once a week for discussing and resolving complaints in a student court format. The rule was as follows: you may complain about anything or anyone at school, including the teacher and the principal, but you must put it in writing, date it, and include your name on it if you want it discussed. Complaints that were illegible or had too many misspellings or grammatical errors were thrown out. This had the added effect of giving problem students extra writing practice. And yes, students did complain in writing about me as their teacher. In the student court, they assigned consequences, such as go talk out the problem with the offended party or take a time out. On occasion, students would voice a complaint about me so the court would appoint certain students to write my wife a letter about my behavior in class. My wife would reply that she had sent me to bed early that night or thanked them for keeping her informed of my behavior and said she would appreciate periodic updates on how I was doing. This had a marvelous effect on the classroom as a whole. If a student became frustrated with something I was doing, he or she could say, "I'm taking you to court." It was a good barometer for me to know when I was pushing it too hard. We also established that students could not use the complaint system to shame another person or to get out of doing regular work.

Over time, one of the students suggested that we should include written positive compliments. This allowed students a safe, indirect way to say nice things to one another. We opened each session of student court by reading compliments about how José had been helpful on a particular project or that Jackie had done a fabulous job on an assignment. This writing-classroom culture built a sense of community as students complimented one another on a regular basis. It also showed them what being authors meant. I really knew the system was working when I began to see "memos" from students appear on my desk, requests or suggestions for upcoming projects or units of study. The students also got into the habit of voicing their concerns by writing the school administration and me. They learned that a well-written letter had the power to change the way things worked around the school community.

Use and Create Media

It is virtually impossible to write about the "latest thing" in a book because of how fast hardware and software move into obsolesce. Nevertheless, some things remain constant. No matter what tool is used, no matter what software is applied, all media requires quality content. Therefore, the focus of this discussion of using and creating media will be more about developing, managing, delivering, and archiving content than a particular new tool. By content, I mean information and experiences that are delivered via some form of media. Content can be discussed online through threaded discussion boards and presented online in digital newsletters.

Some free media delivery systems have shown staying power. Wikispaces .com (www.wikispaces.com) is a viable website for educators to manage and display work whether it is a scanned piece of original artwork, a digital photograph, a short movie clip, or a text-based document. A more sophisticated instrument, at the time of writing this book, is Edublogs.org (edublogs.org), a blogging site exclusively dedicated to educational content. Edublogs.org provides all the features of Wikispaces.com plus threaded discussions, podcasting, digital newsletters, embedding of wikis, social network links, and so forth. Schools and universities use it, including Cornell and Stanford Universities. Edublogs.com prides itself on being safe and secure for students and teachers.

Now back to delivering content. What do you put on a wiki or a blog site? There are two current forms of delivering information and experiences I would like to consider: online threaded discussions and digital newsletters.

Online threaded discussions are features built into wiki and blog sites. Generally, the manager of a site sets up a discussion forum by posting a topic.

Participants can initiate their own discussion threads or contribute to another participant's thread. A discussion thread is a line of responses to one person's comment. Another feature of an online discussion is that it allows participants to not only write comments but also attach documents, pictures, or links to other websites. Online discussions are helpful for intermediate stage ELLs because they are not required to write lengthy passages, the focus is more on content than conventions, they can post visuals, and they can model their writing on the examples of their peers. Teachers can participate in the discussion to provide models for conventional writing and key vocabulary. Each posting identifies the user, so teachers can observe and evaluate the current writing needs of the participants.

The other way to deliver content that I recommend is to return to the concept of a newsletter. I like the idea of creating a digital newsletter for level 3 ELLs because it allows them to use pictures and movies, to write brief passages about information or experiences, and to be highly collaborative in doing so. Collaborative projects increase the social interaction that intermediate stage ELLs need in order to develop fluency in the language. A newsletter can be factual or fictional, poetry or prose. It can be thematic or topical. It can be hard copy or digital, low-tech or high-tech depending on the level of expertise brought to the project. A newsletter format is something everyone can get their heads around regardless of their level of technical expertise. Here are some guidelines for developing digital newsletters:

◆ Establish editorial groups with assigned roles (editor, graphic/layout designer, writers).
◆ Require that all editorial group members contribute a written piece, including the editor and graphic/layout designer.
◆ Keep the editorial groups to a manageable size (four to six students per group).
◆ The editor acts as a liaison between the editorial group and the teacher. The editor is responsible for accuracy and conventions and for writing an introductory piece and an opinion piece.
◆ The graphic/layout designer is responsible for formatting articles, inputting pictures and video clips, and inserting discussion features. He or she is also responsible for writing one or more articles.
◆ Writers propose and contribute articles, poetry, faux advertisements, and interviews. They also initiate and follow online discussions. Allow for freelance writers to contribute to multiple groups, particularly for those students who struggle to collaborate with group projects.
◆ Encourage students to keep written passages short and include visuals.
◆ Decide on a unifying theme to focus group work.
◆ The first time, make a single newsletter with each editorial group responsible for a page. Once the class becomes familiar with the tools, each editorial group can produce its own newsletter.

◆ Insert a discussion board into the newsletter to obtain feedback on the articles.

◆ Go forth and digitally publish. If you struggle to figure out how to use the media tools, rely on the students. You will find that your students don't struggle much at all with using the tools.

Common Core State Standards for Listening and Speaking and Intermediate English Language Learners

This section provides specific examples of ways to apply the appropriate strategies for early intermediate stage ELLs within the following grade ranges: K–2 (Figure 6.6), 3–5 (Figure 6.8), 6–8 (Figure 6.10), and 9–12 (Figure 6.11). Although the suggested strategies are applicable across grade levels, they will look different within grade ranges. The following examples at each grade range demonstrate the unique features of instruction and accommodation using the suggested strategies. Additionally, the following section is intended to be exemplary rather than comprehensive.

Note to Readers: If you are a middle-school or high-school teacher, you may wish to skip ahead to your grade range at this point.

Figure 6.6 Common Core State Standards for Listening and Speaking: K–2

Kindergarten	1. Participate in collaborative conversations with diverse partners about *kindergarten topics and texts* with peers and adults in small and larger groups. a) Follow agreed-upon rules for discussions (e.g., listening to others and taking turns speaking about the topics and texts under discussion). b) Continue a conversation through multiple exchanges. 2. Confirm understanding of a text read aloud or information presented orally or through other media by asking and answering questions about key details and requesting clarification if something is not understood. **a) Understand and follow one- and two-step oral directions.** 3. Ask and answer questions in order to seek help, get information, or clarify something that is not understood.
Grade 1	1. Participate in collaborative conversations with diverse partners about *grade 1 topics and texts* with peers and adults in small and larger groups. a) Follow agreed-upon rules for discussions (e.g., listening to others with care, speaking one at a time about the topics and texts under discussion). b) Build on others' talk in conversations by responding to the comments of others through multiple exchanges. c) Ask questions to clear up any confusion about the topics and texts under discussion.

	2. Ask and answer questions about key details in a text read aloud or information presented orally or through other media. **a) Give, restate, and follow simple two-step directions.** **3.** Ask and answer questions about what a speaker says in order to gather additional information or clarify something that is not understood.
Grade 2	**1.** Participate in collaborative conversations with diverse partners about *grade 2 topics and texts* with peers and adults in small and larger groups. a) Follow agreed-upon rules for discussions (e.g., gaining the floor in respectful ways, listening to others with care, speaking one at a time about the topics and texts under discussion). b) Build on others' talk in conversations by linking their comments to the remarks of others. c) Ask for clarification and further explanation as needed about the topics and texts under discussion. **2.** Recount or describe key ideas or details from a text read aloud or information presented orally or through other media. **a) Give and follow three- and four-step oral directions.** **3.** Ask and answer questions about what a speaker says in order to clarify comprehension, gather additional information, or deepen understanding of a topic or issue.

Strategies for Comprehension and Collaboration, Grades K–2

Conduct a Speedy Interview Rotation of Story Characters

A speedy interview rotation is a combination of elements to guide and foster collaborative conversations. First, it is a series of short interviews in a small-group setting. Each member of the small group is assigned a role as a character from a story that the whole class has read. The small groups sit in circles, and the teacher guides the whole class from the front of the room. The size of the small groups depends upon the number of story characters the teacher wants to deal with.

Once the groups are set and each group member has been assigned a role as a story character, review questions that can be asked about a character in an interview format. Either project on a screen or display on a poster a variety of questions to ask. Use a selection of aesthetic questions referred to in Figure 6.2. Model asking one of the story characters a question. Review rules for raising hands and listening while others are talking. Select the first story character to be interviewed and the order of the subsequent interviews. To add fun to the interview session, include props and costuming so that the children can play the roles of the characters as they are being interviewed.

Now the speedy part comes into play. Set an egg timer for three minutes. Tell students to begin to ask questions and listen to the story character as he or she shares thoughts about what he or she did in the story. After the three-minute timer rings, switch to the next character to be interviewed by the group. Continue around the group until all of the participants have been interviewed.

Follow up the speedy interview rotation with a whole-class reflection on what they learned about each character. Write students' responses on a poster with the corresponding character's picture on display to initiate a character study of each character from the story. Consider the following sequence:

♦ Monday: Conduct the speedy interview rotation and discuss what students learned about one of the characters.
♦ Tuesday: Discuss as a whole group what students learned about two more characters.
♦ Wednesday: Discuss two more characters.
♦ Thursday and Friday: Have each student write about one character and draw a picture of the character to display. Students can refer to the posters you used to record interview information.

Create a "How-to" Knowledge Base for Demonstrating Directions

This standard calls for understanding step-by-step directions and use of other media. Providing and following directions involves sequencing, using command-form verbs, and knowing "how to" do something. I recommend creating a knowledge base and posting it on a wiki or a blog site. A knowledge base is simply a collection of "how to" directions. Sets of directions could be as simple as those for making a peanut butter sandwich or drawing a picture of a face.

Begin by demonstrating a set of directions for some action. Write each step on a sentence strip and display the strips on a sentence strip holder to maintain their order. For example:

Here's how to make a delicious peanut butter sandwich.
Step 1: Place two slices of bread on a cutting board.
Step 2: Spread peanut butter on one slice of bread.
Step 3: Spread jelly or honey on the other slice of bread.
Step 4: Place the jelly slice on top of the peanut butter slice.
Step 5: Eat your sandwich.

Have the students act out the steps with you as you demonstrate each step. Point out the features of each direction, including using numbered steps, a colon for punctuation, and a command verb at the start of each sentence. Keep the number of steps to a minimum. For fun, switch the order of the sentence strips to demonstrate that the sequence of the directions is crucial to making a sandwich. Kindergarten children will manipulate the sentence strips orally, but first and second graders at this stage can work together to write a set of directions. Each would get a sentence strip to write a step of directions.

Enter the set of directions on a page of a wiki or a blog. Include pictures of each step, but when taking pictures, focus on the hands of the children doing the action. For reasons of privacy and security, do not include their faces in the pictures. As the knowledge base grows, the sets of directions on a wiki can become

Figure 6.7 Wh- Question Bank

Who?	Who did it? Who saw it?
What?	What happened? What is going on?
When?	When did this start? When did this end? When did this happen?
Where?	Where did they go? Where are they now? Where is it in the book?
Why?	Why, do you think, did this happen? Why did she do it?
How?	How did you do that? How often does that happen?

a computer center activity. During group rotations, students can view the wiki, select a set of directions, and read and act out the directions with a partner.

Display a Wh- Question Bank

To facilitate gathering details by asking questions, create a question bank to display in the classroom (Figure 6.7). Use a large sheet of paper to make a six-column question bank. Head each column with a wh- question.

You can add to this dynamic display as new questions arise. Encourage students to offer new questions; you might even reward students with class points for contributing new questions to the question bank. During class discussions or interviews, ask students to refer to the question bank for help in formulating questions to ask. You could ask pairs of students to practice asking each other questions after reading a section from a story or an informational text.

Figure 6.8 Common Core State Standards for Listening and Speaking: Grades 3–5

Grade 3	1. Engage effectively in a range of collaborative discussions (one-on-one, in groups, and teacher-led) with diverse partners on *grade 3 topics and texts*, building on others' ideas and expressing their own clearly. a) Come to discussions prepared, having read or studied required material; explicitly draw on that preparation and other information known about the topic to explore ideas under discussion. b) Follow agreed-upon rules for discussions (e.g., gaining the floor in respectful ways, listening to others with care, speaking one at a time about the topics and texts under discussion). c) Ask questions to check understanding of information presented, stay on topic, and link their comments to the remarks of others. d) Explain their own ideas and understanding in light of the discussion.
	2. Determine the main ideas and supporting details of a text read aloud or information presented in diverse media and formats, including visually, quantitatively, and orally.
	3. Ask and answer questions about information from a speaker, offering appropriate elaboration and detail.

Grade 4	1. Engage effectively in a range of collaborative discussions (one-on-one, in groups, and teacher-led) with diverse partners on *grade 4 topics and texts*, building on others' ideas and expressing their own clearly. a) Come to discussions prepared, having read or studied required material; explicitly draw on that preparation and other information known about the topic to explore ideas under discussion. b) Follow agreed-upon rules for discussions and carry out assigned roles. c) Pose and respond to specific questions to clarify or follow up on information, and make comments that contribute to the discussion and link to the remarks of others. d) Review the key ideas expressed and explain their own ideas and understanding in light of the discussion. 2. Paraphrase portions of a text read aloud or information presented in diverse media and formats, including visually, quantitatively, and orally. 3. Identify the reasons and evidence a speaker **or media source** provides to support particular points.
Grade 5	1. Engage effectively in a range of collaborative discussions (one-on-one, in groups, and teacher-led) with diverse partners on *grade 5 topics and texts*, building on others' ideas and expressing their own clearly. a) Come to discussions prepared, having read or studied required material; explicitly draw on that preparation and other information known about the topic to explore ideas under discussion. b) Follow agreed-upon rules for discussions and carry out assigned roles. c) Pose and respond to specific questions by making comments that contribute to the discussion and elaborate on the remarks of others. d) Review the key ideas expressed and draw conclusions in light of information and knowledge gained from the discussions. 2. Summarize a written text read aloud or information presented in diverse media and formats, including visually, quantitatively, and orally. 3. Summarize the points a speaker **or media source** makes and explain how each claim is supported by reasons and evidence, **and identify and analyze any logical fallacies.**

Strategies for Comprehension and Collaboration, Grades 3–5

Use Collaborative Story Interviews to Foster Collaborative Discussions

Collaborative story interviews combine small-group and whole-group interaction. The process involves every member of the class regardless of language level. The purpose of the activity is to have everyone share a story, vote on a particular story to explore, and have the story emerge via an interview process. The following procedure describes how to conduct collaborative story interviews.

Procedure

♦ Organize the class into equal-sized small groups of four to six students.
♦ Number each member in order (1, 2, 3, 4, and so on).
♦ Tell students they will have one minute each to tell their stories.
♦ Set a timer for one minute.
♦ Begin with student 1.
♦ After one minute, follow with student 2.
♦ Repeat the sequence with each student in the group until all students have had a chance to tell their stories. All student groups are doing this simultaneously.
♦ Ask students in each group to vote on the most interesting or compelling story for the group.
♦ Ask each group to give a title to its selected story.
♦ Write the story titles on the board—one from each group.
♦ Have the entire class vote on which story they want to hear about.
♦ Have the student who told the selected story move to an interviewee's chair at the front of the room.
♦ Ask the rest of the students to formulate wh- questions to ask about the story.
♦ Conduct the interview as exclusively oral, or guide students in writing down the interviewee's responses. Students can then arrange the responses in the form of a story as a homework assignment.

Use Software to Develop Oral Presentations

Presentation software is a generic term for any number of tools from computer-housed software to cloud-based programs such as Prezi (prezi.com). Prezi has several unique features that make it a viable tool for students to use for making presentations. First, although one could spend money on enhanced versions of the cloud-based program, Prezi provides a highly adequate free version for educators. Second, because it is cloud-based, students can work on it in class, at home, or at a library without specialized software as long as they have adequate Internet access. Third, the website is highly intuitive. There are short demonstration videos, sample presentations, and even digital "cheat sheets" that make usage instructions quite easy. Furthermore, there is a single tool for presentation development, called a "zebra." It controls inserting text and pictures, zooming in and out, and creating animated pathways and layout style. The zebra is easy to maneuver and much more intuitive than trying to remember in which dropdown menu a particular command might be located, as with so many conventional software programs.

Students may develop presentations about story or a story character, a historical event or an important person, or a current event or particular issue in a debate or show steps to an experiment. The presentation may be used while students speak to a topic or run automatically for others to view on their own time.

Prezis, unlike PowerPoint presentations, consist of more than linear slides. Picture something similar to an architect's drawing table. On this virtual plane, text, drawings, pictures, and even movie clips are arranged. A Prezi follows a pathway set up by the presenter, which zooms over to points of the presentation. It zooms in, out, and back again, according to a specific pathway. Prezis can be highly engaging, but caution students about building Prezis that have too much motion; some viewers might experience vertigo.

Use a Modified Version of a Venn Diagram to Compare Two Speakers

Invite two guests to speak to the class about the same topic. Select speakers who have differing views. When they speak, encourage the students to take notes about the important ideas addressed. After the guests speak, open the class to discussion questions with particular emphasis on asking about the similarities and differences of the two arguments, including the differences and similarities of source material. Follow with having students work in pairs to create a Venn diagram about the unique aspects of each speaker's arguments and the similarities between the two speakers.

Traditional formats for Venn diagrams—intersecting circles—are fine for representing data visually but work poorly for recording written descriptions of differences and similarities. That is because the center section tends to be an inadequate space for writing sentences. I recommend that teachers use a simple three-column table that provides ample room for writing overlapping similarities. Figure 6.9 (below) is an example of a three-column Venn diagram.

Figure 6.9 Three-Column Venn Diagram

Speaker 1 Ideas and Sources	Similar Ideas and Sources	Speaker 2 Ideas and Sources

Figure 6.10 Common Core State Standards for Listening and Speaking: Grades 6–8

Grade 6	1. Engage effectively in a range of collaborative discussions (one-on-one, in groups, and teacher-led) with diverse partners on *grade 6 topics, texts, and issues,* building on others' ideas and expressing their own clearly. a) Come to discussions prepared, having read or studied required material; explicitly draw on that preparation by referring to evidence on the topic, text, or issue to probe and reflect on ideas under discussion. b) Follow rules for collegial discussions, set specific goals and deadlines, and define individual roles as needed. c) Pose and respond to specific questions with elaboration and detail by making comments that contribute to the topic, text, or issue under discussion. d) Review the key ideas expressed and demonstrate understanding of multiple perspectives through reflection and paraphrasing. 2. Interpret information presented in diverse media and formats (e.g., visually, quantitatively, orally) and explain how it contributes to a topic, text, or issue under study. 3. Delineate a speaker's argument and specific claims, distinguishing claims that are supported by reasons and evidence from claims that are not.
Grade 7	1. Engage effectively in a range of collaborative discussions (one-on-one, in groups, and teacher-led) with diverse partners on *grade 7 topics, texts, and issues,* building on others' ideas and expressing their own clearly. a) Come to discussions prepared, having read or researched material under study; explicitly draw on that preparation by referring to evidence on the topic, text, or issue to probe and reflect on ideas under discussion. b) Follow rules for collegial discussions, track progress toward specific goals and deadlines, and define individual roles as needed. c) Pose questions that elicit elaboration and respond to others' questions and comments with relevant observations and ideas that bring the discussion back on topic as needed. d) Acknowledge new information expressed by others and, when warranted, modify their own views. 2. Analyze the main ideas and supporting details presented in diverse media and formats (e.g., visually, quantitatively, orally) and explain how the ideas clarify a topic, text, or issue under study. 3. Delineate a speaker's argument and specific claims, **and attitude toward the subject,** evaluating the soundness of the reasoning and the relevance and sufficiency of the evidence.
Grade 8	1. Engage effectively in a range of collaborative discussions (one-on-one, in groups, and teacher-led) with diverse partners on *grade 8 topics, texts, and issues,* building on others' ideas and expressing their own clearly. a) Come to discussions prepared, having read or researched material under study;

explicitly draw on that preparation by referring to evidence on the topic, text, or issue to probe and reflect on ideas under discussion. b) Follow rules for collegial discussions and decision-making, track progress toward specific goals and deadlines, and define individual roles as needed. c) Pose questions that connect the ideas of several speakers and respond to others' questions and comments with relevant evidence, observations, and ideas. d) Acknowledge new information expressed by others, and, when warranted, qualify or justify their own views in light of the evidence presented.

2. Analyze the purpose of information presented in diverse media and formats (e.g., visually, quantitatively, orally) and evaluate the motives (e.g., social, commercial, political) behind its presentation.

3. Delineate a speaker's argument and specific claims, evaluating the soundness of the reasoning and relevance and sufficiency of the evidence and identifying when irrelevant evidence is introduced.

Strategies for Comprehension and Collaboration, Grades 6–8

Use Online Threaded Discussion to Foster Collaborative Discussions

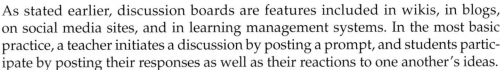

As stated earlier, discussion boards are features included in wikis, in blogs, on social media sites, and in learning management systems. In the most basic practice, a teacher initiates a discussion by posting a prompt, and students participate by posting their responses as well as their reactions to one another's ideas.

The quality of online discussions relies on multiple factors, including the level of interest in the prompt, the level of participation on the part of the teacher, and the quality of the posts. Using discourse analysis, Larson, Boyd-Batstone, & Cox (2009) found that a quality posting in online discussions included one or more of the following elements: telling a personal story, referencing sources or readings, and ruminating about new ideas.

Telling a personal story in an online posting can be as simple as saying something such as "This reminds me of a time when I . . ." or "I had the same experience . . ." It is basically sharing what you know in a narrative form. Teachers can foster personal storytelling in online discussions in a couple of ways. First, tell students prior to the online discussion that you want them to tell their own stories. Second, teachers can invite storytelling when they pose questions to participants such as "Did this ever happen to you? Tell us about it?" or "Does this remind you of another event or experience? What happened?"

Referencing sources and readings in online discussions can be casual or formal. A participant can casually post, "My favorite story character is . . ." or formally post, "In chapter 3, page 47, there is this wonderful idea . . ." Postings can also include embedded links to Internet sites that are sources for the ideas being discussed. Discussion board users can also attach documents, pictures, and other media files.

The third component of a quality post is ruminating about new ideas. This may mean wondering about something in readings or from a video clip that was never considered before. It may mean raising a question of whether what another participant said was a viable idea or not. It could also mean rethinking previously held assumptions.

Clear guidelines from teachers foster quality online postings from students. I recommend stating in the first prompt that for the first post, students are to write about their own ideas; then they may find two or three other participants to respond to. Be clear that an "I agree" or a "good point" response is not a quality posting. Insist that students tell their own stories, reference sources and readings, or ruminate about ideas. They are welcome to disagree with other participants, even the teacher; but they must be courteous and justify their thinking.

◼ Use Cameras and Video Editing Software to Produce Digital Stories

Digital storytelling is easier than ever but it's not without its complications. Given the ubiquitous use of video cameras in so many forms, everyone is capturing their lives on video. But before discussing video production, I need to address software compatibility, video size and bandwidth, and privacy concerns.

Even though the software for video editing and production may be embedded in very affordable cameras and included on almost every computer, there is little standardization across the field. Therefore, it is hard to predict which editing software will work with any particular brand of camera. Try out cameras with your computer software before launching into a video production project.

There is also the secondary issue of the size of videos and the availability of space for housing them. It is vital to consider how the videos will be archived and managed once they are made. A short video clip can take up a tremendous amounts of space—200MB to 2GB—on a computer drive or a website. To upload a video to a wiki or blog, its initial size will most likely need to be reduced. Compressing videos is part of the import-export process. Reducing the size of a video through compression takes time, so allow 30 minutes to an hour to compress each video. If you have a free account with YouTube.com (youtube .com), you can utilize its video compression software for clips of up to six to ten minutes in length. Compressing video using YouTube software does not publish the clip to a public site. It simply reduces the size so that the clip is ready to upload to a wiki, a blog, or a site of your choice.

One other consideration with video production is permissions. In schools, legal permissions must be obtained before pictures of children may be displayed on Internet-based sites. I advise every educator to avoid problems by establishing a policy of never including pictures of children's faces in video productions. Video clips may use slide-show features of representations, drawings, and illustrations or just shots of a child's hand doing something. Keep parents and administrators well informed of the videos that are being produced. Avoid uploading videos to public websites at all cost—use only password-protected sites such as Edublogs.org.

Given those considerations, student production of short video clips involves all aspects of language arts, including listening, speaking, reading, writing, and visually representing. Some possible projects could be reinterpreting a story from a book, enhancing an interview of a guest with pictures and scrolling text, showing the steps in a science experiment, or retelling a historical event.

Design a Digital Newsletter That Includes an Opinion Page

The standards call for summarizing and analyzing a source. Students who contribute to an opinion page in a digital newsletter address the standards in multifaceted ways. Begin by selecting a topic that calls for diverse opinions; you want to publish opposing points of view in the newsletter. Oppositional stances will naturally call for questioning the quality of an opponent's source material. Organize students into pro and con groups about a topic. Guide their research and discuss their citing various source materials to justify their thinking. Post the initial opinions on the digital newsletter page in a wiki or blog. Include a discussion board at the end of the newsletter so that individuals can voice their opinions.

Figure 6.11 Common Core State Standards for Listening and Speaking: Grades 9–12
Note: Readers will see that the following standards for high-school students are very similar from grade to grade with only minor differences. Further, the standards are multifaceted and complex. An English language learner at level 3, the intermediate stage, though limited, can be expected to actively participate in all standards.

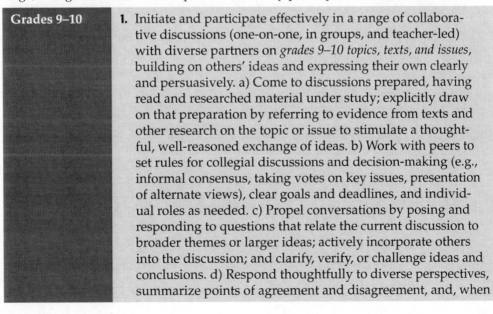

| Grades 9–10 | 1. Initiate and participate effectively in a range of collaborative discussions (one-on-one, in groups, and teacher-led) with diverse partners on *grades 9–10 topics, texts, and issues*, building on others' ideas and expressing their own clearly and persuasively. a) Come to discussions prepared, having read and researched material under study; explicitly draw on that preparation by referring to evidence from texts and other research on the topic or issue to stimulate a thoughtful, well-reasoned exchange of ideas. b) Work with peers to set rules for collegial discussions and decision-making (e.g., informal consensus, taking votes on key issues, presentation of alternate views), clear goals and deadlines, and individual roles as needed. c) Propel conversations by posing and responding to questions that relate the current discussion to broader themes or larger ideas; actively incorporate others into the discussion; and clarify, verify, or challenge ideas and conclusions. d) Respond thoughtfully to diverse perspectives, summarize points of agreement and disagreement, and, when |

	warranted, qualify or justify their own views and understanding and make new connections in light of the evidence and reasoning presented. 2. Integrate multiple sources of information presented in diverse media or formats (e.g., visually, quantitatively, orally) evaluating the credibility and accuracy of each source. 3. Evaluate a speaker's point of view, reasoning, and use of evidence and rhetoric, identifying any fallacious reasoning or exaggerated or distorted evidence.
Grades 11–12	1. Initiate and participate effectively in a range of collaborative discussions (one-on-one, in groups, and teacher-led) with diverse partners on *grades 11–12 topics, texts, and issues*, building on others' ideas and expressing their own clearly and persuasively. a) Come to discussions prepared, having read and researched material under study; explicitly draw on that preparation by referring to evidence from texts and other research on the topic or issue to stimulate a thoughtful, well-reasoned exchange of ideas. b) Work with peers to promote civil, democratic discussions and decision-making, set clear goals and deadlines, and establish individual roles as needed. c) Propel conversations by posing and responding to questions that probe reasoning and evidence; ensure a hearing for a full range of positions on a topic or issue; clarify, verify, or challenge ideas and conclusions; and promote divergent and creative perspectives. d) Respond thoughtfully to diverse perspectives; synthesize comments, claims, and evidence made on all sides of an issue; resolve contradictions when possible; and determine what additional information or research is required to deepen the investigation or complete the task. 2. Integrate multiple sources of information presented in diverse formats and media (e.g., visually, quantitatively, orally) in order to make informed decisions and solve problems, evaluating the credibility and accuracy of each source and noting any discrepancies among the data. 3. Evaluate a speaker's point of view, reasoning, and use of evidence and rhetoric, assessing the stance, premises, links among ideas, word choice, points of emphasis, and tone used.

Strategies for Comprehension and Collaboration, Grades 9–12

Appoint Students as Peer Group Moderators for Online Threaded Discussions

In the previous middle-school section, I discussed the use of online threaded discussions. I provided an overview and suggested some components of quality online discussion postings. Those components are telling personal stories, referencing sources and readings, and ruminating about ideas. Those components apply across grade levels; however, to increase the complexity of the language used for online discussions, assign discussion leaders to virtual small groups.

Setting up groups for an online discussion board is quite easy. Begin with a prompt but then insert the first postings as "Group 1 Responses," "Group 2 Responses," and so forth. Assign students to specific groups, and ask them to respond only within their group's threaded postings. Also assign one or more student moderators to lead each group's discussion. You monitor the moderators.

Peer group moderators in online discussions have the following responsibilities:

♦ Initiate the discussion with an introductory or provocative posting.
♦ Ask clarifying questions about unclear postings.
♦ Encourage all group members to share their ideas.
♦ Compare differing points of view.
♦ Summarize the main points of the discussion for the whole class.

Evaluate the Quality of Information in and Sources for Digital Newsletters

Call on students to question the quality of the arguments in digital newsletters based on the strengths or weaknesses of the sources. The strength of Internet source material can be evaluated according to the quality of the authorship, the publishing body, and the currency of the source material. Authorship on the Internet can sometimes be hidden. Anonymous or hidden authors are suspect as quality sources. If it is difficult to identify the author of a piece, the source may not be credible. Further, authors who are frequently cited by other credible authors have been vetted by their own scholarly community. Google offers a free app called Citation Gadget (code.google.com/p/citations-gadget) that lets you see how often an author is cited and then supplies a search for each article that was cited.

Publishing body refers to the format and content of the publisher of the sources. Some indicators of a quality published source include whether a site is published by a nonprofit group (.org) or a government sponsored agency (.gov), which tend to be stronger sources. Sites identified as .com tend to be weaker sources because their primary function is to sell, and their standards may not be as rigorous as .org or .gov standards. For example, if you are discussing laws regarding access for disabled veterans, the most credible site with regard to laws is a .gov site. Along similar lines, consider whether the publisher is recognizable. Is the online information coming from recognized leaders in the field or from an unknown group? Another indication of quality publishing is the number of references or other sources that a site provides. If a comprehensive list of references is included, then you can be assured of the site's credibility.

Currency of a source is more than just finding the most recent publication, although up-to-date information plays a very important role. The source must

Figure 6.12 Evaluating Source Material

Criteria	Strong Sources	Weak Sources
Authorship	Clearly identified author More information about the author is linked to the source. Other sources cite this author.	Unsigned or anonymous Little to no information about the author is provided. The author is not cited elsewhere as a credible source.
Publishing Body	Is it a .org or .gov site? Is it a recognized publishing group? Comprehensive list of references	Is it a .com site? Is it selling something? There is no homepage or publishing group. Few references
Currency of Work	Recently published Foundational or core source Accurate and well applied statistical information	Out-of-date source Marginal reference to core ideas Inaccurate or poorly applied statistical information

Source: Adapted from John Hopkins University Library guidelines (guides.library.jhu.edu/content.php?pid=198142&sid=1665954)

be up-to-date, but it should also be core to the topic. For example, an article by Albert Einstein or John Dewey was not written in the last five decades, but their ideas may be core or seminal to a current topic. In addition, attend to the accuracy and applicability of any statistical information cited in articles. I recently read an article published by a reputable source—none other than the Harvard Graduate School of Education—that said women comprised 57 percent of the university population. Then the authors dubiously claimed that therefore, men were bored with education. (LeGuillou, 2011, p. 12). The statistic (57 percent) was most likely accurate, but its application was inappropriate. Beware of numbers as well how they are applied.

The tool in Figure 6.12 (above) can help students evaluate the relative strength of source material from Internet sources.

Evaluate the Content of Online Discussion Postings

Earlier in this chapter, I've addressed using online discussion in a variety of ways. Now let's look at using a rubric for evaluating the quality of online postings (Figure 6.13). First, let me state that assigning a grade to every posting in a threaded discussion is not a good use of a teacher's time. It is often much more efficient to give the rubric to peer group moderators to evaluate a group's overall quality of discussion. In addition, simply having a rubric helps clarify for students the expectations for posting information or experiences online.

Figure 6.13 Rubric for Evaluating the Quality of Online Discussion Postings

Criteria	4	3	2	1
Rumination	Posed a new idea or developed an opinion in depth	Opinion stated clearly	Opinion not clearly stated	Little or no evidence of rumination
Storytelling	Provided vivid personal examples or story to give context to the topic	Provided personal examples or story related to the topic	No use of personal examples or story	Unrelated personal examples or story, off-topic
Evocative	Justified reasoning or use of metaphorical thinking that encouraged responses	Interesting idea or metaphor posed with some justification	Argument without justified reason	Uninteresting ideas, poses no responses
Reference, Resource	Appropriately cited relevant ideas beyond the assigned readings	Appropriately referenced class lectures, notes, material, or readings	No citation or references	Inaccurate citation or misapplied reference

Source: Larson, Boyd-Batstone, and Cox (2009)

7

Level 4: The Early Advanced Stage and Common Core Listening and Speaking

Language development is no small undertaking. It takes as long as three to four years to develop a language at the advanced level. Basic communication skills can rapidly develop on a virtually involuntary basis, given the right environment, because the human brain is hardwired for communication. However, advanced language skills, required to perform cognitively demanding and linguistically complex tasks, develop over time with essential academic supports and quality teaching. Early advanced stage ELLs are comfortable in English within familiar realms, which I will refer to as "comfort zones." When ELLs attempt to function outside their language comfort zones, their proficiency becomes somewhat reduced. The goal, then, for ELLs at this stage is to increase the number of academic areas in which they feel fluent and comfortable using English. This means using many of the previously noted strategies plus inserting strategies that push ELLs to use increasingly complex language in cognitively demanding situations.

As with the previous chapters, instructional strategies and activities for early advanced stage ELLs align with the Common Core State Standards for Listening and Speaking according to the following grade level ranges: K–2, 3–5, 6–8, and 9–12. Readers may also note some similarities with the Common Core aligned strategies between early advanced and advanced stages in this and the following chapter. There are nuanced differences between early advanced and advanced stages. Many of the strategies are the same, but complexity is enhanced at the advanced stage.

Early Advanced English Language Learners and Their Comfort Zones

English language learners at the level 4, early advanced, stage demonstrate the ability to operate competently at grade level when dealing with familiar material. As long as they are operating within a comfort zone, they are highly proficient listeners, speakers, readers, and writers. By comfort zones, I mean those topics, spheres of information, and experiences that are familiar to the English language learner. For example, a high-school English teacher from the greater Los Angeles area, who was teaching creative writing to predominantly Mexican American ELLs, complained to me that he was having trouble getting his students to write more than a paragraph about anything. I asked him if he had ever heard about the dreaded Mexican *chupacabra* (see Figure 7.1, below). The *chupacabra* is the legendary creature that preys on animals and terrifies children throughout the Americas. The name literally means "goat sucker" (from the Spanish, *chupar*, to suck, and *cabra*, goat). Everyone that I have ever talked to from Latin America, and Mexico in particular, has not only in-depth knowledge about this creature but also unique stories about a family member's rumored encounter with the *chupacabra*.

I suggested the topic not because of its gruesome nature but because I was certain that every one of the high-school students in that room would have knowledge of the subject and a wealth of family stories about encounters with the mythic creature. I knew that the students in this class, and in particular the ELLs at this stage, would have plenty to write about a shared experience that was very familiar and vivid. I could not wait to hear back from the English teacher after he asked his students to interview their family members about the *chupacabra*. They were to bring the recorded interviews back to class to use when writing about close encounters with the *chupacabra*.

Two weeks later, the English teacher enthusiastically gushed that he had never before, in more than a dozen years of teaching creative writing, had such an overwhelming response to a suggested topic. Initially, the students did not believe that they had been given such an outrageous assignment. This had never been raised as a legitimate topic for any course ever before in their experiences

Figure 7.1 The Legendary Chupacabra

in school. It was always relegated to home conversations outside the boundaries of school. They wrote pages and pages in class, based on the interviews. The excitement buzzed as they squealed in fear and delight as students shared their stories. There was something visceral about it.

Consider the topic. It is very familiar, culturally embedded, and based upon shared experiences—and it has juice! Of course, in a range of academic areas, not all topics fit those criteria. But the point here is that students used more complex language in order to conduct more complex tasks such as interviewing, summarizing, and writing compelling stories because they were operating inside their comfort zone. They understood what they were communicating, so the language flowed fluently and easily. Using their comfort zone, the English teacher was able to teach the less exciting components of writing, such as how to convert a run-on sentence into a simpler complete sentence or how to structure a story that flowed from the beginning, through the middle, and to a climactic ending. The next instructional phase was to apply the newly acquired academic language structures to new aspects of the literary learning, such as comparing and contrasting the *chupacabra* to other mythical creatures, such as the Beast of Bodmin Moor, or Sir Arthur Conan Doyle's *Hound of the Baskervilles*. In learning theory, this exemplifies the practice of the Zone of Proximal Development (ZPD), as theorized by Vygotsky (1996). In brief, instruction is mediated as it moves from new learning to the familiar, the comfort zone, to greater capacity to take on new learning and begins the cycle again.

What benefits early advanced ELLs is to begin instruction with the familiar in order to move them forward into new learning. Start in the comfort zone, and push the boundaries to increase that zone or to add comfort zones in other areas. This type of dynamic pushes students to conduct complex language tasks, such as presenting their writing to others, actively listening and asking questions of one another, debating topics, and thinking metaphorically and theoretically while drawing on their own culturally embedded understanding of the world.

Adding comfort zones involves initiating all new subject areas with explicit instruction of new vocabulary, using realia and visuals to provide linguistic experiences, not just looking up definitions of decontextualized words. Adding comfort zones means making the curriculum come alive with role-playing, walking to significant sites students are learning about, and reinterpreting events through media. The learners cannot be passive; they must actively be involved in listening, thinking and questioning, speaking, reading, writing, and visually representing the curriculum. Do nothing for students that they can do for themselves. Have them outline the lesson on the board. Have them produce plays. Have them read to the class. Have them write invitations to speakers to come to class, and have them generate interview questions. In accordance with Vygotsky's (1996) Zone of Proximal Development, ELLs are moving toward becoming more self-directed learners. The teacher mediates instruction by inviting ELLs to be more actively involved in their learning. As early advanced ELLs increase their familiarity with topics, they become more skilled, autonomous learners who are ready to take on new learning.

Figure 7.2 Helpful Strategies and Unhelpful Practices

Helpful Strategies	Unhelpful Practices
Beginning instruction with the familiar—comfort zone	Disregarding the value of teaching from a place that is familiar to the students
Including frequent checks for understanding, such as asking students to paraphrase what was just discussed	Getting upset at students who say they don't understand
Using comfort zones to teach new material and skills	Pushing students outside their comfort zones without academic supports (e.g., telling students to debate a topic without demonstrating the discourse style and structure of debate formats)
Continuing to introduce new concepts with explicit and concrete vocabulary instruction	
Continuing to show visuals and real objects that give clues and images about the instruction	Teaching new material without making connections to prior knowledge or experiences
Actively involving students in the learning—having them perform tasks such as outlining subject matter on the board for the teacher	Falsely assuming that early advanced ELLs no longer need academic supports
Asking students to debate topics	Reducing learning to lectures that put students into a passive learner mode
Assigning interviews of people about topics of familiar and new learning	Making all assignments individual and solitary, thus neglecting the need for social interaction in order to develop oral fluency about a topic
Inviting students to teach one another about familiar topics as a test review	
Using culturally embedded topics or events as a means to showing similar examples in other cultural settings	Devaluing questions that on the surface may appear off topic but in reality reflect a cultural understanding of an event or topic
Going back to a familiar experience of learning and making a comparison to illustrate a point when student appear confused	Neglecting to tap into the cultural perceptions the students hold about an event or topic
Drawing on the cultural understandings that students bring to the learning	

Figure 7.2 (above) summarizes the helpful strategies and unhelpful practices for early advanced ELLs.

The Early Advanced Stage English Language Learner

Identifiable language behaviors of a student at the early advanced stage are listed below. Let's look at some of these in more detail.

◆ Appears to be orally fluent
◆ Uses limited academic vocabulary and language
◆ Needs to attain grade level reading and writing in academic areas
◆ Analyzes, compares, and contrasts.

Appears to Be Orally Fluent

Early advanced ELLs can fool teachers. The ELLs know how to appear engaged and interested even when they are confused and do not understand the material. As stated earlier, they are quite fluent within familiar topics. Once outside those familiar realms, they tend to function more as intermediate stage speakers. To their advantage, they know immediately when the material moves outside their comfort zones. Given the opportunity, they will tell teachers when they don't understand what is being taught if the classroom environment honors students who raise their hands and say, "I don't understand." If teachers get upset with students who raise that concern, they risk spending time teaching incomprehensible material and not finding out that the point was missed until they see test results.

A better approach is to build frequent checks for understanding into the routine of instruction. This does not need to be an elaborate process. It can be as simple as paraphrasing the learning. Teachers can ask students to pause and tell their seat partner in their own words what they are studying. I like to add to the exercise by requesting, "OK, now that you have paraphrased the learning for each other, tell me what your neighbor told you." This request has several impacts on the learning. First, it pushes students to actively listen to each other. Second, it holds students accountable to actually talk with each other about the subject at hand. Third, it forces students to consider whether their partner gave them an accurate paraphrase of the learning.

Uses Limited Academic Vocabulary and Language

At this stage of language development, the focus of instruction should be on developing academic vocabulary and language skills. Early advanced ELLs can help with this too. They no longer depend exclusively upon the teacher to explicitly teach all vocabulary. They should have developed some skills at this point to find out the meanings of words for themselves. A quality use for such handheld Internet devices as tablets is to have students look up academic vocabulary and find related images or illustrations of words.

Early advanced ELLs also need to be reminded to use academic discourse when writing reports, critiques, or reviews. A helpful tool for this is to have students make posters for classroom display about academic language usages. Picture a poster that explains what a run-on sentence is, shows an example, and provides several options for how to convert the sentence into a coherent complete sentence. Further, posters can identify, define, and provide examples of conventional use of the various parts of speech. When such posters are displayed, early advanced ELLs are reminded on a daily basis of how to use academic language appropriately in their writing.

Needs to Attain Grade Level Reading and Writing in Academic Areas

This student behavior is an observation of what early advanced ELLs need, although it reads more like a recommendation. To experience success in school and society, ELLs need to take an active role in their academic language development. Given a quality learning environment, ELLs can move virtually involuntarily from beginning to intermediate stages of proficiency. The language complexity required at those earlier levels permits ELLs to function at a basic needs level. However, advanced levels of proficiency are demanded to succeed in schooling and beyond. Consequently, early advanced ELLs, with the systemic support of the entire educational community, must take initiative to develop complex academic language skills.

The following section explains in more detail the recommended strategies to address the need to attain grade level reading and writing in academic areas.

Recommended Strategies for Early Advanced Language Learners Defined

In this chapter, level 4, early advanced stage, language behaviors and instructional applications are provided. The instructional applications are as follows:

◆ Shift focus from oral to written language development
◆ Expand study and learning skills
◆ Provide formal grammar instruction
◆ Use SDAIE strategies

The above list of recommended strategies is found on the CALL assessment tool. The strategies address the overarching need of early advanced ELLs to develop their academic language skills and vocabulary. From the student side of the equation, early advanced ELLs must focus on developing their written language, expanding their study skills, and studying grammar formally. Teachers foster this learning by using Specially Designed Academic Instruction in English, a collection of strategies that shelter content-based learning.

Shift Focus from Oral to Written Language Development

At this stage of language development, ELLs are quite fluent in oral language production. They can speak to a range of topics within their comfort zone. They know how to ask questions and hold discussions in order to obtain information and share ideas. From a teacher's perspective, they function quite well in the classroom. However, the area of greatest need is to develop greater facility with print literacy, reading more-complex material and expanding their writing across genres. For example, so much of ELLs initial writing experiences at earlier levels tend to be in a narrative style. They write about what they like and experience using first person. Certainly, their use of narrative needs to be enhanced, but they also need to begin to write in other styles, such as reviews, critiques, and reports. The use of writing frames can be very helpful at this point. On page 141, for example, is a writing frame for the high-school level that facilitates composing an abstract from a research article (see Figure 7.14). Well-constructed writing frames can guide ELLs in forming and ordering sentences to match particular discourse styles and genres.

Expand Study and Learning Skills

Early advanced ELLs need to concentrate on how to become successful students. This is not a uniquely linguistic task, per se; it is something all students need to learn. It is particularly helpful at this stage of language development because of the shift from oral to written language development. Further, it sends the message that teachers want students to succeed as scholars in whatever field they choose. Teachers of early advanced ELLs are no longer satisfied with minimum compliance and covering the class material. We communicate to students and parents that, whether or not they choose to go on to higher education, they will be prepared to succeed on that pathway.

Students at this stage need to gain access to appropriate Internet-based search and referencing tools, they need to learn how to structure their time for study, and they need to know what to highlight from their textbook readings. The classroom teacher would do well to invest time, particularly at the beginning of the school year, showing early advanced ELLs how to use a calendar to organize their time, set goals, and note assignments with due dates, and how to structure a plan for studying over a several-day period with notes, texts, and media resources. Additionally, it would help students to practice holding study groups during class time, under the supervision of the teacher, so students can rehearse how to have a successful experience outside class. A wonderful resource for study skills is the Latino Scholars Network (www.hsf .net/uprogram_toolkit.aspx?id=2146), which includes suggestions for different learning styles, study tools kits, and more. Figure 7.3 (page 126) shows a list of success factors for study groups; you could post this list in your classroom.

Provide Formal Grammar Instruction

Providing formal grammar instruction is appropriate at this stage of language development because of the shift in focus from oral to written language development. Even though there are negative connotations associated with the notion of "formal grammar instruction," there are many ways to make grammar instruction very interesting and engaging, not the least of which is an endless supply of Internet sources, including YouTube videos, grammar related blogs, and images of examples of poor grammar usage that can be used for instructional purposes. Consider keeping a classroom display of pictures of examples of poor grammar with corrected versions next to each picture. They can be quite funny reminders of how to use an apostrophe, when to use *their*, and appropriate use of punctuation.

Students also need to learn to separate the world of text messaging, which has a much more lax approach to spelling, grammar, and punctuation, from writing in the academic world. It won't help to rant against casual texting, but the teacher needs to hold expectations for writing that identify and correct texting phrases in academic writing. Purdue University created and maintains an open source website for a range of writing tools, including grammar, punctuation, and research, called the Purdue Online Writing Lab (OWL) (owl.english .purdue.edu/owl). Using this resource, students can make their own posters

Figure 7.3 Study Group Success Factors

Attend all class and section meetings. Everyone's participation is key.

Choose a regular and recurring meeting time to limit confusion and disappointment.

Have clearly stated goals for each study session and be sure to allot enough time for each level of the learning process.

If no one wants to lead the group, rotate the leadership and keep the responsibilities balanced.

Stay focused and on task. Everyone's time is precious. Nothing is worse than allotting study time and then not getting any studying done.

Stay in close communication with each other if something comes up.

Always remind each other of expectations and assignments so there are no disappointments or setbacks.

Be accountable to one another at all times. Encourage each other and remind everyone how important it is to be prepared for each study session.

Establish ground rules for staying focused and getting the work done at the very beginning of your study group formation.

Do not continue to include people who do not meet the expectations of the group.

Make sure everyone understands the material before moving on.

Be sure to consult with your professor or your TA if there are questions that come up during a study session. Report back to the group so everyone is clear about the correct answers.

It can also be very effective to have more than one study group get together to help each other study before a mid-term or a final exam.

Source: Latino Scholars Network, a project of the Hispanic Scholarship Fund (www.hsf.net/uprogram _toolkit.aspx?id=2146)

about various aspects of writing in an academic world and display them around the classroom. A poster would include several elements, including the name of the topic, a definition of what it is, rules for usage, and examples of mistakes as well as models for correct usage. Figure 7.4 (page 127) offers a suggested format for a poster.

Use SDAIE Strategies

Until the late 1980s, linguists dominated much of the literature regarding teaching language minority students. However, the need to teach subject matter while developing language proficiency among ELLs changed the nature of the field. The concept of content area instruction that also develops language proficiency can be traced to Alfredo Schifini (1985). He was a middle school history and geography teacher in East Los Angeles and has since become a professor of

Figure 7.4 Sample Punctuation Poster

Punctuation: Apostrophe
Rules
An apostrophe has three uses:

1. to form possessives of nouns
2. to show the omission of letters
3. to indicate certain plurals of lowercase letters

Fix the following phrases and sentences:	*Examples of Correct Usage*
Eat at Joes	Possessives The boy's hat = the hat of the boy.
I wont do it.	three days' journey = journey of three days
His' favorite book	Omission of letters don't = do not I'm = I am he'll = he will
Shes a fan.	who's = who is shouldn't = should not
The childrens' show	didn't = did not
	Certain plurals Mind your p's and q's.

renown in the field. His middle-school classes were comprised predominantly of English language learners who were struggling to read and write at grade level, which compounded the challenge of maintaining grade level competence in content areas such as history and geography. As skilled teachers often do, through trial and error, Schifini came up with a set of effective strategies that had the dual purpose of making content area material more comprehensible while developing academic language. This notion has evolved over time.

Diane Sobol (1995) is credited with coining the term *Specially Designed Academic Instruction in English* (SDAIE), which specifically defined an approach to teaching ELLs built on the foundation of sheltered instruction with some aspects informed by best practices in bilingual education. Her unique contribution was to emphasize the linguistic value of providing primary language support in conjunction with the sheltering strategies for teaching content area literacy. Primary language support could take the form of previewing a lesson in students' home languages, teaching the body of the lesson in English, and reviewing the lesson in the students' home languages. Other forms of primary language support include permitting students to discuss and question the content of the

Figure 7.5 Components of Specially Designed Academic Instruction in English (SDAIE)

Lessons: Teachers organize lessons to support an overarching topic or theme. The topic or theme may extend across curricular areas.

Content Standards-Based Instruction: Teachers design assessments and instruction that are informed by the standards. The standards identify what all students should "know and be able to do" at specific grade levels.

Content Driven Instruction: Teachers differentiate instruction according to proficiency levels. Although SDAIE was designed for intermediate level fluency and above, students at early proficiency levels need to be accommodated.

Vocabulary: Teachers explicitly instruct students on content-related vocabulary. Vocabulary is visually represented to increase understanding. Materials include real objects, models, pictures, graphic organizers, tools, and media resources.

Tapping Prior Knowledge: Students recall prior experiences: "Think back to a time when . . ." Previous learning: "Remember when we studied . . ."

Grouping Strategies to Increase Social Interaction: Teachers use a variety of groupings to increase communication: pairs, small groups, cooperative learning.

Problem Posing: Teachers pose problems that engage all learners in collaborative projects and in-depth thinking.

Total Physical Response: Students act out the meanings of words in order to use both hemispheres of the brain.

Language Experience Approach: Teachers write students' words on chart paper for collaborative writing projects.

Source: Alfredo Schifini (1985)

instruction in their own languages in small groups, using cognates strategically, using key phrases during the instructional time in the students' home languages for clarification purposes, and defining key terms in the home languages. The value of primary language support is an essential feature of quality instruction for English language learners. See Figure 7.5 (above) for a list of the components of SDAIE.

Building on the notion of providing content area instruction and language development simultaneously, Vogt, Echevarria, and Short (2004, 2007) developed the sheltered instruction observational protocol (SIOP) as a model for planning for instruction and observing instruction. This popular model reduced the emphasis on primary language support that SDAIE promoted but continued the use of the teaching strategies, maintaining the dual intention of teaching content while developing language.

Figure 7.5 Components of Specially Designed Academic Instruction in English (SDAIE) (*continued*)

Journaling: Students maintain a daily rhythm of writing for personal expression and practice.

Concept Mapping: Students use an array of graphic organizers to make explicit connections between subjects, contrasting ideas, cause and effect, and work flow.

Writing Process: Students move through the range of writing from envisioning ideas, drafting, revising, editing, final drafts, and publication.

Primary Language Support: Applying the students first language (L_1) as a means of support for comprehension includes primary language usage for previewing lesson vocabulary and content, use of L_1 for clarification, lesson content taught in English, and review of the lesson outline and key terms, and discussion of deeper questions that students may not be able to articulate in English. Other forms include using the primary language during English instruction for clarification purposes, using cognates strategically, and allowing students to discuss and ask questions in their own language.

Multicultural/Cross-Cultural Strategies: Whenever possible, teachers select resources that reflect the cultural fabric of the group; study content in terms of multiple perspectives. Students share their experiences regarding the learning and conduct "we-search" projects to study their own lives and community.

Accommodate "Teacher Talk": Teachers use slower speech, mirror back to students their words with model speech, use cognates frequently, and use students' primary languages for clarification purposes.

Assessment: Teachers use formative and classroom-based assessment to inform ongoing instruction (anecdotal records, teacher observation); summative assessment after the fact to analyze how we did (project evaluation, rubric, exams).

Common Core State Standards for Listening and Speaking and Advanced English Language Learners

This section provides specific examples of how to apply the appropriate strategies for early advanced stage ELLs within the following grade ranges: K–2 (Figure 7.6), 3–5 (Figure 7.8), 6–8 (Figure 7.10), and 9–12 (Figure 7.12). Early advanced approaches differ slightly from those for advanced ELLs. Sometimes, the same strategies apply to both with only a nuance of difference. You will find in this and the following chapter that similar strategies will be discussed, but the depth and complexity of the language usage will differ according to language level.

Note to Readers: If you are a middle-school or high-school teacher, you may wish to skip ahead to your grade range at this point.

Figure 7.6 Common Core State Standards for Listening and Speaking: K–2

Kindergarten	1. Participate in collaborative conversations with diverse partners about *kindergarten topics and texts* with peers and adults in small and larger groups. a) Follow agreed-upon rules for discussions (e.g., listening to others and taking turns speaking about the topics and texts under discussion). b) Continue a conversation through multiple exchanges. 2. Confirm understanding of a text read aloud or information presented orally or through other media by asking and answering questions about key details and requesting clarification if something is not understood. **a) Understand and follow one- and two-step oral directions.** 3. Ask and answer questions in order to seek help, get information, or clarify something that is not understood.
Grade 1	1. Participate in collaborative conversations with diverse partners about *grade 1 topics and texts* with peers and adults in small and larger groups. a) Follow agreed-upon rules for discussions (e.g., listening to others with care, speaking one at a time about the topics and texts under discussion). b) Build on others' talk in conversations by responding to the comments of others through multiple exchanges. c) Ask questions to clear up any confusion about the topics and texts under discussion. 2. Ask and answer questions about key details in a text read aloud or information presented orally or through other media. **a) Give, restate, and follow simple two-step directions.** 3. Ask and answer questions about what a speaker says in order to gather additional information or clarify something that is not understood.
Grade 2	1. Participate in collaborative conversations with diverse partners about *grade 2 topics and texts* with peers and adults in small and larger groups. a) Follow agreed-upon rules for discussions (e.g., gaining the floor in respectful ways, listening to others with care, speaking one at a time about the topics and texts under discussion). b) Build on others' talk in conversations by linking their comments to the remarks of others. c) Ask for clarification and further explanation as needed about the topics and texts under discussion. 2. Recount or describe key ideas or details from a text read aloud or information presented orally or through other media. **a) Give and follow three- and four-step oral directions.** 3. Ask and answer questions about what a speaker says in order to clarify comprehension, gather additional information, or deepen understanding of a topic or issue.

Strategies for Comprehension and Collaboration, Grades K–2

Participate in a Role-Play About Listening and Asking Clarifying Questions

To apply initial academic skills, young children need to rehearse asking appropriate questions. To develop skill in asking clarifying questions, students need to know what kinds of questions to ask, how to ask the questions, and the appropriate times to ask. Role-playing scenarios can address all three areas. They do not need to be elaborate or lengthy; it just requires a little pre-planning. Before instruction, write selected questions on large sentence strips. Then meet with two or three students and give each of them a question as a model for the rest of the class. Inform the students ahead of time that you are going to demonstrate how to ask clarifying questions. Then teach a portion of the lesson, pause, and invite each of the prepared students to ask his or her question. Have students hold their sentence strips so that the whole class can see them. Post the selected questions on the board in front of the class. Next, organize the group into role-playing pods (one teacher, two to three students). The teacher role player reteaches the section, and each student practices asking a question. Figure 7.7 (below) shows some selected clarifying questions that may be used.

Lead a Prepared Total Physical Response Activity

A Total Physical Response (Asher, 1969) activity is a series of commands that call on participants to act out the meanings of words. Think of the game Simon Says without the aspect of trying to catch participants off guard. The teacher models the movements with the students. James Asher developed the TPR approach as a therapeutic response to people who had suffered trauma to one hemisphere of the brain. They could picture and act out the meanings of words but struggled to verbalize words. He found that this technique of using meaningful gestures was also a helpful strategy for second language acquisition. It is particularly useful for ELLs at beginning and early intermediate stages of proficiency. I return to the activity here with a different application in mind. Have early advanced students play the role of teacher and lead groups in demonstrating the numbered commands on the poster.

Figure 7.7 Sample Clarifying Questions

What does that mean?
Can you be more specific?
Why do you think that?
Can you share some examples?
What do you really mean?
Can you clarify that for me?

Conduct the TPR activity as follows:

♦ Make a poster with a collection of numbered commands. The commands may lead a group in acting out a scene from a story, drawing a face, or performing a collection of unrelated actions.
♦ Organize the class into TPR practice pods (one leader and three to four participants).
♦ Ask the leaders to read the commands aloud and to demonstrate the appropriate actions.
♦ Have them lead their assigned groups in each command.

The value of this activity is that it places the early advanced ELL in a more public role of using language on behalf of a group. It involves listening, speaking, reading, and representing the commands to classmates. Another benefit is that many classrooms are made up of students from a range of language levels. This activity allows lower level ELLs to participate in an appropriate activity while early advanced ELLs lead in the same activity. In other words, you get two for one.

▉ Prepare Questions for a Class Interview of a Guest Speaker

This activity is an assignment for early advanced ELLs to be completed prior to having a guest speaker come to class. They must prepare ahead of time to interview the class guest. They will need to read some background information about the topic and the speaker, if available. From their notes about the subject, they formulate questions and prepare to ask the questions while the speaker is present. Some basic guidelines for formulating interview questions follow.

♦ Consider what you want to learn.
♦ Select the type of wh- questions that will give you the answers you are looking for.
♦ Think about how to follow up your initial questions.
♦ Avoid asking a question simply to display your knowledge of the subject.

Figure 7.8 Common Core State Standards for Listening and Speaking: Grades 3–5

| Grade 3 | 1. Engage effectively in a range of collaborative discussions (one-on-one, in groups, and teacher-led) with diverse partners on *grade 3 topics and texts*, building on others' ideas and expressing their own clearly. a) Come to discussions prepared, having read or studied required material; explicitly draw on that preparation and other information known about the topic to explore ideas under discussion. b) Follow agreed-upon rules for discussions (e.g., gaining the floor in respectful ways, listening to others with care, speaking one at a time about the |

topics and texts under discussion). c) Ask questions to check understanding of information presented, stay on topic, and link their comments to the remarks of others. d) Explain their own ideas and understanding in light of the discussion.

2. Determine the main ideas and supporting details of a text read aloud or information presented in diverse media and formats, including visually, quantitatively, and orally.

3. Ask and answer questions about information from a speaker, offering appropriate elaboration and detail.

Grade 4

1. Engage effectively in a range of collaborative discussions (one-on-one, in groups, and teacher-led) with diverse partners on *grade 4 topics and texts*, building on others' ideas and expressing their own clearly. a) Come to discussions prepared, having read or studied required material; explicitly draw on that preparation and other information known about the topic to explore ideas under discussion. b) Follow agreed-upon rules for discussions and carry out assigned roles. c) Pose and respond to specific questions to clarify or follow up on information, and make comments that contribute to the discussion and link to the remarks of others. d) Review the key ideas expressed and explain their own ideas and understanding in light of the discussion.

2. Paraphrase portions of a text read aloud or information presented in diverse media and formats, including visually, quantitatively, and orally.

3. Identify the reasons and evidence a speaker **or media source** provides to support particular points.

Grade 5

1. Engage effectively in a range of collaborative discussions (one-on-one, in groups, and teacher-led) with diverse partners on *grade 5 topics and texts*, building on others' ideas and expressing their own clearly. a) Come to discussions prepared, having read or studied required material; explicitly draw on that preparation and other information known about the topic to explore ideas under discussion. b) Follow agreed-upon rules for discussions and carry out assigned roles. c) Pose and respond to specific questions by making comments that contribute to the discussion and elaborate on the remarks of others. d) Review the key ideas expressed and draw conclusions in light of information and knowledge gained from the discussions.

2. Summarize a written text read aloud or information presented in diverse media and formats, including visually, quantitatively, and orally.

3. Summarize the points a speaker **or media source** makes and explain how each claim is supported by reasons and evidence, **and identify and analyze any logical fallacies.**

Strategies for Comprehension and Collaboration, Grades 3–5

▌ Participate in Panel Discussions

Participation in a panel discussion requires that the participants come prepared as experts in their topic. Use a form of jigsaw to set roles for each panel member. In other words, choose a chapter from a textbook. Organize the chapter into sections, and assign each panel member a different section to read. Panel members should prepare to respond to questions from the panel moderator and the class. Thus, each panel participant will have unique knowledge about the subject. With early advanced ELLs, the teacher could operate as the moderator of the panel.

With each panel member having specialized knowledge, the moderator could either ask the questions or simply facilitate the discussion as the panel members respond to questions from the rest of the class. Maintaining wall displays of types of questions will ensure that students have sample questions to draw on for the discussion.

Another way to organize the panel is to have participants take stances on a particular issue. This debate format fosters lively discussion, and unlike the jigsaw format, which involves specialized knowledge, all parties have the same sources but differing opinions.

▌ Outline and Paraphrase a Text

Outlining and paraphrasing text go hand in glove. Particularly with informational text, outlining a passage functions to ensure the inclusion of the important details. Paraphrasing allows students to explain the main points of a text in their own words. There is also an interpretive aspect to paraphrasing that may update language from an earlier stage.

This is a good place to teach the differences between quotations (exact copying of a text with citations), summarizing (brief rendering of a text's main points with citations), and paraphrasing (using your own words to interpret a text with citations included). Note that for each aspect of deriving information from a text, an accurate citation is required.

Figure 7.9 Steps in a Structured Debate

> Step 1: Take a turn to present your side of a question.
> Step 2: Summarize the opponent's points of view for the whole group.
> Step 3: Question and respond to each other.
> Step 4: Provide a final statement as a rebuttal.

Structured Debate: Present, Summarize, Question, Rebut

Structured debate formats address the main considerations of the Common Core at this point. The standard calls for asking and answering questions, identifying reasons or evidence for a point of view, and summarizing the points of a text or speaker. Within a structured debate format, all of the above can be successfully addressed. Using a simplistic debate structure does not follow classic formats for debating. The overarching purpose is to engage ELLs in the process of questioning, summarizing, analyzing, and rebutting. The simple format for a debate shown in Figure 7.9 (page 134) can facilitate those skills.

Figure 7.10 Common Core State Standards for Listening and Speaking: Grades 6–8

Grade 6	
	1. Engage effectively in a range of collaborative discussions (one-on-one, in groups, and teacher-led) with diverse partners on *grade 6 topics, texts, and issues*, building on others' ideas and expressing their own clearly. a) Come to discussions prepared, having read or studied required material; explicitly draw on that preparation by referring to evidence on the topic, text, or issue to probe and reflect on ideas under discussion. b) Follow rules for collegial discussions, set specific goals and deadlines, and define individual roles as needed. c) Pose and respond to specific questions with elaboration and detail by making comments that contribute to the topic, text, or issue under discussion. d) Review the key ideas expressed and demonstrate understanding of multiple perspectives through reflection and paraphrasing.
	2. Interpret information presented in diverse media and formats (e.g., visually, quantitatively, orally) and explain how it contributes to a topic, text, or issue under study.
	3. Delineate a speaker's argument and specific claims, distinguishing claims that are supported by reasons and evidence from claims that are not.
Grade 7	
	1. Engage effectively in a range of collaborative discussions (one-on-one, in groups, and teacher-led) with diverse partners on *grade 7 topics, texts, and issues*, building on others' ideas and expressing their own clearly. a) Come to discussions prepared, having read or researched material under study; explicitly draw on that preparation by referring to evidence on the topic, text, or issue to probe and reflect on ideas under discussion. b) Follow rules for collegial discussions, track progress toward specific goals and deadlines, and define individual roles as needed. c) Pose questions that elicit elaboration and respond to others' questions and comments with relevant observations and ideas that bring the discussion back on topic

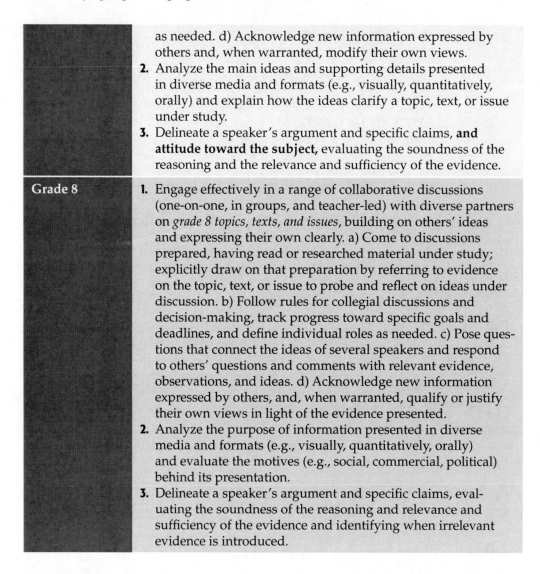

as needed. d) Acknowledge new information expressed by others and, when warranted, modify their own views.

2. Analyze the main ideas and supporting details presented in diverse media and formats (e.g., visually, quantitatively, orally) and explain how the ideas clarify a topic, text, or issue under study.

3. Delineate a speaker's argument and specific claims, **and attitude toward the subject,** evaluating the soundness of the reasoning and the relevance and sufficiency of the evidence.

Grade 8

1. Engage effectively in a range of collaborative discussions (one-on-one, in groups, and teacher-led) with diverse partners on *grade 8 topics, texts, and issues,* building on others' ideas and expressing their own clearly. a) Come to discussions prepared, having read or researched material under study; explicitly draw on that preparation by referring to evidence on the topic, text, or issue to probe and reflect on ideas under discussion. b) Follow rules for collegial discussions and decision-making, track progress toward specific goals and deadlines, and define individual roles as needed. c) Pose questions that connect the ideas of several speakers and respond to others' questions and comments with relevant evidence, observations, and ideas. d) Acknowledge new information expressed by others, and, when warranted, qualify or justify their own views in light of the evidence presented.

2. Analyze the purpose of information presented in diverse media and formats (e.g., visually, quantitatively, orally) and evaluate the motives (e.g., social, commercial, political) behind its presentation.

3. Delineate a speaker's argument and specific claims, evaluating the soundness of the reasoning and relevance and sufficiency of the evidence and identifying when irrelevant evidence is introduced.

Strategies for Comprehension and Collaboration, Grades 6–8

Record or Present the Content of a Discussion Group

In effective small-group discussion, each participant has an assigned role. Some roles are more suited to the strengths and needs of an ELL at the early advanced stage than other roles. For example, the group leader, or moderator, may not be the best role for ELLs at this point because of the complexity of language skills required to effectively moderate a group. Some suggested roles for group discussion include the following: leader/moderator, recorder, timekeeper, presenter, and editor. The leader or moderator synthesizes what others are saying and formulates questions based on that synthesis. The recorder notes the main points of the discussion and reflects back to the group what was said. The timekeeper helps keep the group on task for the allotted time. The presenter speaks on behalf of the group to the rest of the class regarding the content of the discussion. The editor reviews the presentation of information for clarity and accuracy.

Although early advanced ELLs may not have the requisite skill set to be effective moderators, there are roles ideally suited for their stage of language development. It is very much within their ability to record what others are saying and to put those ideas on paper in a coherent, logical format. Especially with the help of an editor, they can produce accurate records of discussions. The other role that is well suited for ELLs to play at this stage is the presenter because the presenter works from a prepared script instead of speaking extemporaneously in front of the group.

Narrate a Digital Story Using Storyboards

The corresponding Common Core standard for this section calls for interpretation and presentation of a text using diverse media. ELLs at this stage are well positioned to act as narrators of a text in a digital storytelling format. They are able to rehearse and read a script with a high degree of fluency and accuracy. They may or may not write scripts, but reading them aloud on camera is well within their level of proficiency.

Movie directors use storyboarding techniques to organize their projects. A storyboard frame (Figure 7.11, page 138) can facilitate the development of a script and inform the narrator what is taking place on the screen as the text is being read. Included in each frame of a storyboard can be a quick sketch of the visuals, notations of the durations of visuals, and the lines of text to be narrated.

Vote with Your Feet

Voting with your feet is an activity that follows up reading a text, viewing media, or hearing a speaker on a polemical topic. Basically, it is a way to express an opinion, to discuss one's thinking, and then to engage in persuasion of classmates.

Procedure
1. Arrange the desks in the room so that there are three gathering spots.
2. Label a gathering spot on one side with "Agree," the spot in the center with "Undecided," and the spot on the opposite side with "Disagree."
3. Prepare several polemical statements or ideas, drawn from text the group read, some media students viewed, or a speaker the group listened to.
4. Read aloud to the class one of the polemic statements.
5. Invite the participants to express opinions by saying, "Now vote with your feet."
6. Participants stand by the labeled gathering spot that expresses "Agree," "Undecided," or "Disagree."
7. After students have gathered with like-minded participants, invite them to explain their thinking to one another.

Figure 7.11 Storyboard Sample Frame

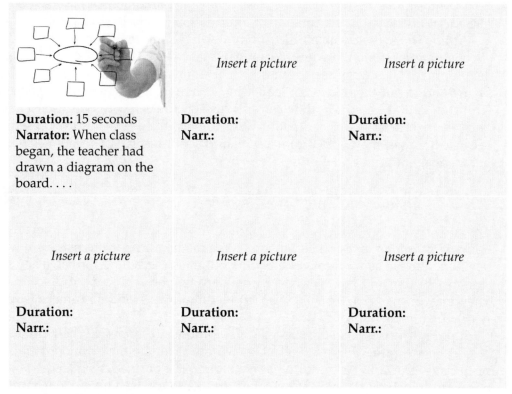

	Insert a picture	*Insert a picture*
Duration: 15 seconds **Narrator:** When class began, the teacher had drawn a diagram on the board. . . .	**Duration:** **Narr.:**	**Duration:** **Narr.:**
Insert a picture	*Insert a picture*	*Insert a picture*
Duration: **Narr.:**	**Duration:** **Narr.:**	**Duration:** **Narr.:**

Source: Created by the author.

8. Ask the participants if anyone changed their minds after discussing their opinions. Invite them to move to another gathering spot if they did change their minds by saying, "Vote with your feet."

9. Ask the participants to find someone with a different opinion and try to persuade him or her to change.

10. Give the participants one last time to vote with their feet and to explain what changed their mind about the issue.

11. Follow up the activity with a written summary of your opinion.

Figure 7.12 Common Core State Standards for Listening and Speaking: Grades 9–12

Note: Readers will see that the following standards for high-school students are very similar from grade to grade with only minor differences. Further, the standards are multifaceted and complex. Nevertheless, an English language learner at level 4, the early advanced stage, can be expected to actively participate in all standards. Further, ELLs at this level can expect to excel given appropriate language supports.

Grades 9–10	1. Initiate and participate effectively in a range of collaborative discussions (one-on-one, in groups, and teacher-led) with diverse partners on *grades 9–10 topics, texts, and issues*, building on others' ideas and expressing their own clearly and persuasively. a) Come to discussions prepared, having read

and researched material under study; explicitly draw on that preparation by referring to evidence from texts and other research on the topic or issue to stimulate a thoughtful, well-reasoned exchange of ideas. b) Work with peers to set rules for collegial discussions and decision-making (e.g., informal consensus, taking votes on key issues, presentation of alternate views), clear goals and deadlines, and individual roles as needed. c) Propel conversations by posing and responding to questions that relate the current discussion to broader themes or larger ideas; actively incorporate others into the discussion; and clarify, verify, or challenge ideas and conclusions. d) Respond thoughtfully to diverse perspectives, summarize points of agreement and disagreement, and, when warranted, qualify or justify their own views and understanding and make new connections in light of the evidence and reasoning presented.

2. Integrate multiple sources of information presented in diverse media or formats (e.g., visually, quantitatively, orally) evaluating the credibility and accuracy of each source.

3. Evaluate a speaker's point of view, reasoning, and use of evidence and rhetoric, identifying any fallacious reasoning or exaggerated or distorted evidence.

Grades 11–12

1. Initiate and participate effectively in a range of collaborative discussions (one-on-one, in groups, and teacher-led) with diverse partners on *grades 11–12 topics, texts, and issues*, building on others' ideas and expressing their own clearly and persuasively. a) Come to discussions prepared, having read and researched material under study; explicitly draw on that preparation by referring to evidence from texts and other research on the topic or issue to stimulate a thoughtful, well-reasoned exchange of ideas. b) Work with peers to promote civil, democratic discussions and decision-making, set clear goals and deadlines, and establish individual roles as needed. c) Propel conversations by posing and responding to questions that probe reasoning and evidence; ensure a hearing for a full range of positions on a topic or issue; clarify, verify, or challenge ideas and conclusions; and promote divergent and creative perspectives. d) Respond thoughtfully to diverse perspectives; synthesize comments, claims, and evidence made on all sides of an issue; resolve contradictions when possible; and determine what additional information or research is required to deepen the investigation or complete the task.

2. Integrate multiple sources of information presented in diverse formats and media (e.g., visually, quantitatively, orally) in order to make informed decisions and solve problems, evaluating the credibility and accuracy of each source and noting any discrepancies among the data.

3. Evaluate a speaker's point of view, reasoning, and use of evidence and rhetoric, assessing the stance, premises, links among ideas, word choice, points of emphasis, and tone used.

Figure 7.13 Analysis of Evidence

Directions: List the items of evidence to analyze. Decide whether the evidence is accurate. Circle Y= yes or N= no. Write brief explanations about how you came to your conclusions. Share your conclusions with the class.

Item 1:

Accurate? Y/N How?	Distorted? Y/N How?	Exaggerated? Y/N How?	Inaccurate? Y/N How?

Item 2:

Accurate? Y/N How?	Distorted? Y/N How?	Exaggerated? Y/N How?	Inaccurate? Y/N How?

Item 3:

Accurate? Y/N How?	Distorted? Y/N How?	Exaggerated? Y/N How?	Inaccurate? Y/N How?

Source: Created by the author.

Strategies for Comprehension and Collaboration, Grades 9–12

Participate in a Group Analysis of Evidence

Early advanced ELLs can fully participate in analyzing evidence in small-group settings. What is helpful for them is to consider the various ways to evaluate evidence. According to the standard, evaluation is based on the degree to which it is accurate, distorted, exaggerated, or inaccurately presented.

The frame in Figure 7.13 can help students analyze evidence. It simply asks them to identify the evidence presented and to describe its degree of accuracy and how they concluded it was accurate, distorted, exaggerated, or inaccurate.

Jigsaw, Write, and Present an Abstract of a Research Study

One way early advanced ELLs can address the 9–12 grade standards is to work as a group to analyze and abstract a selected research article in a jigsaw format. The work sheet on page 141 (Figure 7.14) can help students with the abstracting

Figure 7.14 300-Word Research Abstract Work Sheet

Sentence Prompts
1. Write a sentence or more in each box below according to the prompts provided.
2. Keep the number of words within the suggested range provided for each category.
3. Compile the sentences into a 300-word abstract.
4. Title the abstract with the name of the research project.
5. Present the abstract as a paragraph, poster, or media presentation.

Problem: Begin with a statement of the problem or topic addressed by the research.	*(40–50 words)*
Context: State the context of the research. • *What* is the theoretical background? • *Who* are the action researchers? • *Where*? Location • *Who*? Participant information (number, gender, ethnicity, socio-economic status)	*(50–70 words)*
Methodology: Briefly describe the methodology of the study. • Cite source for methodology. • State the basic steps of the research study.	*(30–60 words)*
Findings: Summarize the principal findings. • Order findings according to the research questions. • Keep it to major findings. • Avoid listing every finding.	*(50–70 words)*
Conclusions: Summarize: • Major conclusions • Recommendations for practice • Recommendations for additional research	*(30–50 words)*

Source: Adapted from Richard Sagor, *The Action Research Guidebook: A Four-Step Process for Educators and School Teams* (Thousand Oaks, CA: Corwin Press, 2005) 163. Print.

process. It is organized into the following sections: problem, context, methodology, findings, and conclusions. In a group of five students, each could take responsibility for one aspect of the research article. Their jobs would be to find the key information requested from the prompt in their assigned sections. They would need to summarize the information into one or two sentences to meet the prescribed word count. Then, as a group, students would combine their sentences into a complete abstract. The final group task would be to present the abstracted research to the rest of the class as a single tightly written paragraph, a poster for display, or an oral report using presentation software. The directions are included on the work sheet. It can be used for a wide-range of research studies, including qualitative and quantitative methodologies.

Participate in a Debate Online

Early advanced ELLs who can participate in a panel discussion are ready to take part in a debate. Develop a topic in class that is worthy of a lively debate. Practice arguing sides in class, and then add the component of conducting an online debate with YouTube's free debate channel, DBateMe (www.youtube.com/user/DBateMe). All that is required is a free YouTube account, a moderator, and a topic worth debating. Online debates have an allotted time frame, so they end once debaters reach the time limit. The moderator sets the rules for the debate. Using DBateMe also creates an archive of the debate so that students can review and score how well they performed. A related resource for teachers is Education World (www.educationworld.com/a_lesson/lesson/lesson304b.shtml). This website provides all the tools needed to develop debate topics, evaluate debates with rubrics, and score debates with prepared scoring sheets.

8

Level 5: The Advanced Stage and Common Core Listening and Speaking

Achieving advanced stage, level 5, proficiency is the ultimate goal of the English language learner. Although a single teacher may want to take credit for having successfully worked with an ELL who attains advanced stage proficiency, the achievement is due in large part to the support of a network of dedicated individuals, including parents and family members, previous teachers, administrators, librarians, and mentors in the community. Ultimately, however, the student deserves credit for such an accomplishment.

Several facets of high-level language development distinguish advanced stage ELLs. They exhibit a high level of skill with language conventions within content area material. For example, it is not unusual for an advanced ELL to successfully edit and proofread a paper written by a native English speaker. Advanced ELLs tend to be excellent spellers because they have had to work hard to figure out the confounding system of orthography in English. For them, the way words are spelled in English had no natural ring or didn't necessarily look right. Spelling rules have so many exceptions that the ELLs literally build their own understanding of English orthography, such as the advanced ELL who told me that the only way he could figure out how to spell *mayonnaise* was to say it aloud to himself in Spanish (mai-yo-nay-se).

Another aspect of language development that distinguishes advanced ELLs is that they display a high level of comfort in casual and formal social settings. Advanced ELLs have learned appropriate behaviors in a range of social settings, including culturally bound, tacit rules of dress and courtesy. They also understand culturally embedded jokes and plays on words. ELLs at the early advanced stage recognize that a joke is being told to a group, understand every word being spoken, and even laugh along with the group, but they may not get the punch line. This marks a difference. Advanced stage ELLs understand the joke, laugh appropriately, and possibly even come back with a related joke.

With their grade level competence and facility in social settings, the key goals for advanced ELLs are to refine language skills and to play active leadership roles in academic settings. Leadership requires an array of complex skills, including organizing programs, moderating panels and group discussions, managing group projects, and editing collaborative publications.

As with the previous chapters, instructional strategies and activities for advanced stage ELLs align with the Common Core State Standards for Listening and Speaking according to the following grade level ranges: K–2, 3–5, 6–8, and 9–12. Readers may note some similarities with the Common Core aligned strategies between early advanced and advanced stages in this and the preceding chapter. There are nuanced differences between early advanced and advanced stages. Many of the strategies are the same but with enhanced complexity at the advanced stage.

Refining Language and Fostering Leadership

I once had a third-grade student named Adriana. She was a highly engaged English language learner and an absolute pleasure to work with. Her parents had the equivalent of a first-grade education from their home country of Mexico, but they were very supportive of her education. Much to her credit, Adriana advanced in her language and academic development and graduated from high school as the valedictorian. She went on to university with a full-ride scholarship to study forensic science. One day out of the blue, during her junior year of university studies, she called me to express appreciation for being her teacher. She told me that even in college, she continued to practice things that she had learned in third grade. I tell this story not to take credit for her success but because I asked her, "Tell me, what helped you succeed? What did we do that was right?"

Adriana paused and began to list a number of instructional practices that had made a difference for her. She expressed an appreciation that I had concentrated on developing her writing skills. Students wrote every day in class and in multiple ways. We spent a significant amount of time revising and editing written work with the intent of making it public for others to read. Although we expected first drafts to be filled with errors, disjointed thoughts, and code switching, we insisted that final drafts be logical and that spelling, grammar, and punctuation be 100 percent correct for writing that had gone through the process of drafting, revision, editing, final drafts, and publication. Adriana reminded me that I had invited students to write and illustrate their own books, which we had bound and placed in the school library for others to check out. Her class had contributed dozens of self-published books.

Something else Adriana expressed appreciation for was that I had looked to the students as a great resource of knowledge. Aesthetic questions, such as "What were you thinking?," invited their perceptions into discussions. If we were unsatisfied with something we read, we wrote the publisher to complain. If we wanted to find out more information, I asked students to find the information and report to the group. She reminded me of one of her classmates, Eddie, who said that he liked being in class because "Mr. BB saw that I had ideas." I used their thinking as the source for their writing. Adriana realized that she had gained a voice for her thoughts in class. Along those lines, she reminded me of how she used to leave notes on my desk with suggestions for what she wanted to learn. I referred to them as memos from students, which I treated very seriously. The curriculum did not blindly dictate what we studied in class. Of course, I followed curriculum guidelines, but there was flexibility to incorporate the knowledge and intentions of the students.

What Adriana shared with me aligns with the research on teacher knowledge in culturally and linguistically complex classrooms. According to a review of the research literature conducted by Paris and Ball (2009), there is tremendous value in connecting teacher knowledge and the knowledge that culturally and linguistically nondominant students bring to the classroom.

> Because many of the teachers in these [culturally and linguistically complex] classrooms come from very different cultural, linguistic, and socioeconomic backgrounds than their students, it is imperative that they become generative in . . . curricular problem-solving skills, so they can link the knowledge they have with the knowledge their students bring into the classroom. (p. 392)

Teachers bring official knowledge to the classroom such as knowing the curriculum, content standards, and writing conventions. Students, on the other hand bring to the classroom their diverse cultural perceptions and funds of knowledge (Moll & Gonzalez, 1994). When those two sources of knowledge are tapped, creative problem-solving and critical thinking take place. In practice, the teacher and students enter into a dialogue about their learning; they listen to each other's perceptions and pose problems to each other about the learning. They invite alternative ways to understand the instructional content into the dialog. Together they begin to figure out how to make the curriculum comprehensible, culturally relevant, and useful for their purposes. Conversely, when the curriculum is treated as a set of dictates to be learned, without regard for student perceptions and knowledge, then creative problem solving and critical thinking are devalued, and the ability to differentiate the curriculum is lost. Therefore, teachers who want to meet the needs of all students should invite their thinking, listen to their ideas, observe their ways of learning, and respond to their strengths, needs, and cultural ways of knowing.

Figure 8.1 summarizes helpful strategies and unhelpful practices for advanced ELLs.

Figure 8.1 Helpful Strategies and Unhelpful Practices

Helpful Strategies	Unhelpful Practices
Placing a strong emphasis on refining writing skills	Reducing the amount of writing because first drafts are too full of errors
Using students as peer editors of one another's writing	Not taking written work through the full writing process because it is too much work
Providing and displaying a uniform system of editorial marks so that all understand their meaning and usage	Falsely assuming that advanced ELLs no longer need linguistic supports
Encouraging leadership opportunities in discussion groups	Using advanced ELLs as "teachers" for other ELLs
Asking advanced ELLs to synthesize what the group is discussing	Teaching the curriculum without adaptations for differentiation
Encouraging leadership roles in problem-solving activities and collaborative groups	Falsely assuming that advanced ELLs cannot take leadership roles with group work
Inviting the cultural perspectives of ELLs into the curriculum	Lowering expectations for ELLs
Discussing with ELLs how to make the curriculum more culturally relevant	Dumbing down the curriculum
Inviting humor in the form of jokes and plays on words	Objecting to humor and joke telling in the classroom
Maintaining high standards for the content and conventions of writing	Reserving higher order skills, such as researching, for only the best students in class
Refining research skills	

The Advanced Stage English Language Learner

Identifiable language behaviors of a student at the advanced stage are listed below. Let's look at some of these in more detail.

- ◆ Comprehends content material
- ◆ Generates discussions
- ◆ Is socially comfortable
- ◆ Reads and writes at grade level

Comprehends Content Material

English language learners at the advanced stage operate at grade level proficiency in language and consequently can readily comprehend grade level content material. Being able to comprehend, however, does not mean understanding reading without supports, such as visuals, vocabulary development activities, and advanced organizers. Curriculum may require little support when it has been presented in the past and is being revisited in more depth. Revisiting previously taught content material requires a quick review of key terms and essential concepts. Additionally, the introduction of new material needs the same kind of vocabulary development activities used at earlier levels. Practicing the use of realia and visuals at all stages of language development is always helpful. Providing initial linguistic support for vocabulary and concepts is a very efficient way to teach. It reduces confusion in the long run. Advanced ELLs, once they recognize the key terms and ideas, are just as capable as their native English speaking counterparts to fully participate in the learning.

Generates Discussions

A benchmark behavior of advanced ELLs is their confidence in initiating discussions and raising questions in class. They can fluently express themselves in front of others and formulate original questions. This is a strategic behavior that teachers can use to foster language development. Asking advanced ELLs to lead group discussions, conduct interviews, and role-play short skits in front of the class are just some of the ways to put them in a place to generate discussions. A key to this behavior is having advanced ELLs generate their own questions. Ideally, they participated in a variety of question and response activities as they developed at earlier stages, so by this level, they know how to pose questions. It is also helpful at this stage to remind advanced ELLs of a *range* of questions so they can avoid always asking the same *types* of questions.

Is Socially Comfortable

An advanced ELL tends to appear comfortable in a variety of social settings. Advanced ELLS use culturally appropriate words and phrases, which shows courtesy. They aren't overly formal or overly familiar but read social settings appropriately.

Humor comes into play here. Advanced ELLs tend to get jokes told in casual group settings. They may even have some fun making up jokes that include plays on words or culturally embedded humor. One famous example took place during the Strategic Arms Limitations Treaty (SALT) negotiations between the Soviet Union and the United States in the summer of 1976. The negotiations were conducted in both English and Russian through interpreters. During an intense negotiating session about defining terms such as *launch weights of missiles*, Boris Klossman, the chair of the United States drafting committee, reiterated for emphasis, "It is the weight of a fully loaded missile at the time of the launch, free of anything attached to it, free of anything attached to it." At which point, Victor Karpov, the Soviet counterpart, broke away from his language interpreter and interjected in English, "But I thought in America that there was no such thing as a *free launch*." (Graham, 2002, p. 72). Karpov made a brilliant play on words from the highly culturally embedded phrase sometimes attributed to the economist Milton Freeman, "There's no such thing as a free lunch." He most definitely was an advanced ELL.

Recommended Strategies for Advanced Language Learners Defined

In this chapter, level 5, advanced stage language behaviors and instructional applications are provided. The instructional applications are as follows:

◆ Expand academic vocabulary
◆ Refine writing skills
◆ Refine research/study skills
◆ Complete complex projects

This short list of appropriate strategies is found on the CALL assessment tool. They are not the only strategies that could be employed, but they correspond to the language behaviors that are unique to ELLs at this stage of language development. As you may have noted from previous chapters, there is a progression of strategies that require increasingly more complex linguistic skills at each stage. This is an additive progression that seeks to keep using the previously described strategies while adding new ones. In other words, the use of realia and visuals, though not mentioned to the same extent in this current chapter, is just as applicable in the advanced stage as any other. Below is a discussion of how to teach using each strategy in more detail.

Expand Academic Vocabulary

I once knew a P.E. teacher who would use only anatomical terminology with his students, and he would insist that they do the same. He wouldn't say, "Touch your *knees*"; he'd say, "Touch your *patellae*." Along the same lines, he'd tell students to "stretch out their *phalanges*" and "move their *thorax* from side to side." The strategy was designed to increase students' fluency with the language of kinesiology. He was actively developing the language of his discipline. At an advanced level, ELLs need to actively increase their use of academic language because the goal is not that they merely survive in school, but that they excel academically. Expanding the use of academic vocabulary applies to all subject areas from literary criticism to mathematics to social sciences to kinesiology. Well-educated people accurately use the language of multiple disciplines to learn and communicate complex ideas.

Refine Writing Skills

Expanding vocabulary and refining writing skills go hand-in-glove. Along with promoting greater fluency with academic vocabulary, teachers must show students how to use transitions, how to structure their writing so that it has a logical flow, and how to communicate in writing for different audiences. Refining writing skills includes learning a greater range of discourse styles including narrative, informational, research reporting, persuasive writing, and critical analysis.

Refine Research/Study Skills

Higher-level skills such as researching and studying are appropriate for instruction at this level. Advanced ELLs require the tools to learn for themselves in order to achieve academically. Skills related to research include learning where to find quality source material, using Internet search engines appropriately, and abstracting essential information from research articles. Study skills include note taking and organizing material for study. In addition, students must learn how to review and identify what is essential and superfluous information. Refining these skills allows advanced ELLs to use a greater range of material and equips them with ways to evaluate content and source material.

Complete Complex Projects

Students at the advanced stage of language proficiency can take complex projects that require pulling teams together, negotiating the best approach to solve a problem, and creating ways to represent their ideas. Complex projects require collaborative efforts that foster high-level language usage. Consider having ELLs at this level take on the role of editors of a newsletter, producers of video productions, group leaders of debate teams, or directors of dramatic presentations. This is the time to challenge ELLs in ways that will stretch their use of language and put them in situations where they will need to guide others with clear and accurate speech.

Common Core State Standards for Listening and Speaking and Advanced English Language Learners

This section provides specific examples of how to apply the appropriate strategies for advanced stage ELLs within the following grade ranges: K–2 (Figure 8.2), 3–5 (Figure 8.4), 6–8 (Figure 8.5), and 9–12 (Figure 8.8). Although the suggested strategies are applicable across grade levels, they will look different within grade ranges. The following examples at each grade range demonstrate the unique features of instruction and accommodation using the suggested strategies. Additionally, the following section is intended to be exemplary rather than comprehensive.

Note to Readers: If you are a middle-school or high-school teacher, you may wish to skip ahead to your grade range at this point.

Figure 8.2 Common Core State Standards for Listening and Speaking: Grades K–2

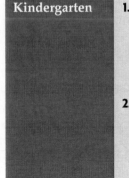

| Kindergarten | 1. Participate in collaborative conversations with diverse partners about *kindergarten topics and texts* with peers and adults in small and larger groups. a) Follow agreed-upon rules for discussions (e.g., listening to others and taking turns speaking about the topics and texts under discussion). b) Continue a conversation through multiple exchanges.
2. Confirm understanding of a text read aloud or information presented orally or through other media by asking and answering questions about key details and requesting clarification if something is not understood. **a) Understand and follow one- and two-step oral directions.** |

	3. Ask and answer questions in order to seek help, get information, or clarify something that is not understood.
Grade 1	1. Participate in collaborative conversations with diverse partners about *grade 1 topics and texts* with peers and adults in small and larger groups. a) Follow agreed-upon rules for discussions (e.g., listening to others with care, speaking one at a time about the topics and texts under discussion). b) Build on others' talk in conversations by responding to the comments of others through multiple exchanges. c) Ask questions to clear up any confusion about the topics and texts under discussion. 2. Ask and answer questions about key details in a text read aloud or information presented orally or through other media. **a) Give, restate, and follow simple two-step directions.** 3. Ask and answer questions about what a speaker says in order to gather additional information or clarify something that is not understood.
Grade 2	1. Participate in collaborative conversations with diverse partners about *grade 2 topics and texts* with peers and adults in small and larger groups. a) Follow agreed-upon rules for discussions (e.g., gaining the floor in respectful ways, listening to others with care, speaking one at a time about the topics and texts under discussion). b) Build on others' talk in conversations by linking their comments to the remarks of others. c) Ask for clarification and further explanation as needed about the topics and texts under discussion. 2. Recount or describe key ideas or details from a text read aloud or information presented orally or through other media. **a) Give and follow three- and four-step oral directions.** 3. Ask and answer questions about what a speaker says in order to clarify comprehension, gather additional information, or deepen understanding of a topic or issue.

Strategies for Comprehension and Collaboration, Grades K–2

Create a Role-Play About Listening and Asking Clarifying Questions

Just as with early advanced ELLs, advanced ELLs can benefit from practice in asking clarifying questions of a speaker. To increase the complexity of the language to meet the needs of advanced ELLs, simply turn over the responsibility of creating a role-play scenario with clarifying questions to the students. Provide a small group of advanced ELLs with the same list of clarifying questions. After teaching a lesson, ask advanced ELLs to create a role-play scenario in which one takes on the role of the teacher giving the lesson and two other students formulate clarifying questions. The student playing the teacher makes up responses to the

Figure 8.3 Sample Clarifying
Questions

What does that mean?
Can you be more specific?
Why do you think that?
Can you share some examples?
What do you really mean?
Can you clarify that for me?

questions from the role-playing students. The skit is conducted orally and lasts no longer than two to three minutes. There is no written assignment included in the activity. Suggestions for clarifying questions are shown in Figure 8.3, above.

Develop and Lead a Total Physical Response Activity

As stated in chapter 7, a Total Physical Response (Asher, 1969) activity is a series of commands that call on participants to act out the meanings of words. It has broad application across language levels. ELLs at earlier stages of language proficiency benefit from TPR because it involves the whole body in demonstrating meaning, and it introduces words at a pre-linguistic level. Advanced ELLs can benefit from developing their own TPR activities to help teach vocabulary to the rest of the class. An appropriate place to insert a TPR activity is at the outset of a presentation to the rest of the class.

TPR Activity
♦ Make a poster with a collection of numbered commands. The commands may lead the group in acting out a scene from a story, drawing a face, or performing a collection of unrelated actions.
♦ Lead the entire group in each command.

Moderate a Class Interview of a Guest Speaker

Another way to encourage an advanced ELL to use a full range of language skills is to invite him or her to moderate a class interview of a guest speaker. The invited speaker may be anyone from an employee at the school to a notable member of the community. Here are some basic guidelines for the moderator to follow:

♦ Write a letter of invitation to the guest. Communicate the intention of the interview. Consider what you want to learn and topics to address.
♦ Coordinate the date, time, location, and duration of the interview.
♦ Recruit a classmate to be the recorder.
♦ Select the type of wh- questions that will give you the answers you are looking for.

- Think about how to follow up your initial questions.
- Initiate the interview with an appropriate overview question.
- Invite class members to ask questions.
- Supply questions when class members are not sure what to ask.
- Summarize what you learned from the interview.

Figure 8.4 Common Core State Standards for Listening and Speaking: Grades 3–5

Grade 3	1. Engage effectively in a range of collaborative discussions (one-on-one, in groups, and teacher-led) with diverse partners on *grade 3 topics and texts*, building on others' ideas and expressing their own clearly. a) Come to discussions prepared, having read or studied required material; explicitly draw on that preparation and other information known about the topic to explore ideas under discussion. b) Follow agreed-upon rules for discussions (e.g., gaining the floor in respectful ways, listening to others with care, speaking one at a time about the topics and texts under discussion). c) Ask questions to check understanding of information presented, stay on topic, and link their comments to the remarks of others. d) Explain their own ideas and understanding in light of the discussion. 2. Determine the main ideas and supporting details of a text read aloud or information presented in diverse media and formats, including visually, quantitatively, and orally. 3. Ask and answer questions about information from a speaker, offering appropriate elaboration and detail.
Grade 4	1. Engage effectively in a range of collaborative discussions (one-on-one, in groups, and teacher-led) with diverse partners on *grade 4 topics and texts*, building on others' ideas and expressing their own clearly. a) Come to discussions prepared, having read or studied required material; explicitly draw on that preparation and other information known about the topic to explore ideas under discussion. b) Follow agreed-upon rules for discussions and carry out assigned roles. c) Pose and respond to specific questions to clarify or follow up on information, and make comments that contribute to the discussion and link to the remarks of others. d) Review the key ideas expressed and explain their own ideas and understanding in light of the discussion. 2. Paraphrase portions of a text read aloud or information presented in diverse media and formats, including visually, quantitatively, and orally. 3. Identify the reasons and evidence a speaker **or media source** provides to support particular points.

Grade 5	1. Engage effectively in a range of collaborative discussions (one-on-one, in groups, and teacher-led) with diverse partners on *grade 5 topics and texts*, building on others' ideas and expressing their own clearly. a) Come to discussions prepared, having read or studied required material; explicitly draw on that preparation and other information known about the topic to explore ideas under discussion. b) Follow agreed-upon rules for discussions and carry out assigned roles. c) Pose and respond to specific questions by making comments that contribute to the discussion and elaborate on the remarks of others. d) Review the key ideas expressed and draw conclusions in light of information and knowledge gained from the discussions. 2. Summarize a written text read aloud or information presented in diverse media and formats, including visually, quantitatively, and orally. 3. Summarize the points a speaker **or media source** makes and explain how each claim is supported by reasons and evidence, **and identify and analyze any logical fallacies.**

Strategies for Comprehension and Collaboration, Grades 3–5

Lead an Expert Panel Discussion

Leading a panel discussion requires deciding on a topic, selecting panel members, and ensuring that they are prepared as experts on their topic. Early advanced ELLs would jigsaw the chapter or topic, but a panel leader is responsible for knowing the entire topic or selected text. The leader is also responsible for assigning sections of a text to each expert panel member.

With each panel member having specialized knowledge, the moderator could ask the questions or simply facilitate the discussion as the panel members respond to questions from the rest of the class. Maintaining wall displays of types of questions can help ensure that students have sample questions to draw on for the discussion.

Another way to organize the panel is to have students take stances on particular issues. This debate format fosters lively discussion, and unlike the jigsaw format, which involves specialized knowledge, all parties have the same sources but differing opinions.

Facilitate a Jigsaw Activity to Outline and Summarize a Text

Another way that advanced ELLs can develop their use of the language and address standard 1 above is to facilitate a jigsaw activity in a small group.

Procedure
- Read a chapter in the text ahead of time, and organize it into logical segments for the jigsaw.
- Assign segments to members of the group to read and present to the group.
- Establish allotted times and monitor pacing of the activity.
- Moderate the presentations back to the group.
- Synthesize the major findings of the group.

Moderate a Debate

Advanced ELLs who can moderate a panel discussion are ready to moderate a debate. Moderating a debate requires multiple language skills, including guiding a discussion, monitoring pacing, practicing objective speech and analysis, summarizing what has been said for the audience, and formulating topics and questions.

Debate Guidelines for Student Moderators
- Maintain a debate format: Ask the party taking the affirmative position to make a statement. Follow with a statement from the party taking a negative position. Ask questions of each party in turn. Allow for rebuttals and final closing remarks.
- Monitor time and pacing: Announce the time limits at the opening. Give each party equal time to speak. Step in and cut off a debater who runs over the time limit.
- Hold the focus of the debate to one question at a time: Avoid confusing the debate with multiple questions or off-topic discussions. Refocus the group by restating the question at hand.
- Give each party the opportunity to make a closing statement: Allow equal time for the closing remarks. Consider mirroring back to each party what he or she said.
- *Consider having the audience score the debate:* EducationWorld.com (www.educationworld.com/a_lesson/lesson/lesson304b.shtml) provides free scoring sheets that can be used for any debate.

Figure 8.5 Common Core State Standards for Listening and Speaking: Grades 6–8

Grade 6	1. Engage effectively in a range of collaborative discussions (one-on-one, in groups, and teacher-led) with diverse partners on *grade 6 topics, texts, and issues,* building on others' ideas and expressing their own clearly. a) Come to discussions prepared, having read or studied required material; explicitly draw on that preparation by referring to evidence on the topic, text, or issue to probe and reflect on ideas under discussion. b) Follow rules for collegial discussions, set specific goals and

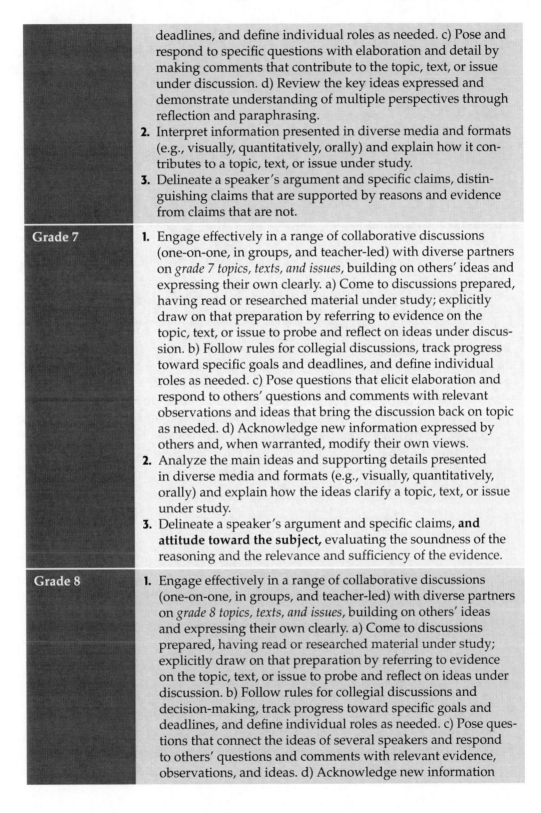

deadlines, and define individual roles as needed. c) Pose and respond to specific questions with elaboration and detail by making comments that contribute to the topic, text, or issue under discussion. d) Review the key ideas expressed and demonstrate understanding of multiple perspectives through reflection and paraphrasing.

2. Interpret information presented in diverse media and formats (e.g., visually, quantitatively, orally) and explain how it contributes to a topic, text, or issue under study.

3. Delineate a speaker's argument and specific claims, distinguishing claims that are supported by reasons and evidence from claims that are not.

Grade 7

1. Engage effectively in a range of collaborative discussions (one-on-one, in groups, and teacher-led) with diverse partners on *grade 7 topics, texts, and issues,* building on others' ideas and expressing their own clearly. a) Come to discussions prepared, having read or researched material under study; explicitly draw on that preparation by referring to evidence on the topic, text, or issue to probe and reflect on ideas under discussion. b) Follow rules for collegial discussions, track progress toward specific goals and deadlines, and define individual roles as needed. c) Pose questions that elicit elaboration and respond to others' questions and comments with relevant observations and ideas that bring the discussion back on topic as needed. d) Acknowledge new information expressed by others and, when warranted, modify their own views.

2. Analyze the main ideas and supporting details presented in diverse media and formats (e.g., visually, quantitatively, orally) and explain how the ideas clarify a topic, text, or issue under study.

3. Delineate a speaker's argument and specific claims, **and attitude toward the subject,** evaluating the soundness of the reasoning and the relevance and sufficiency of the evidence.

Grade 8

1. Engage effectively in a range of collaborative discussions (one-on-one, in groups, and teacher-led) with diverse partners on *grade 8 topics, texts, and issues,* building on others' ideas and expressing their own clearly. a) Come to discussions prepared, having read or researched material under study; explicitly draw on that preparation by referring to evidence on the topic, text, or issue to probe and reflect on ideas under discussion. b) Follow rules for collegial discussions and decision-making, track progress toward specific goals and deadlines, and define individual roles as needed. c) Pose questions that connect the ideas of several speakers and respond to others' questions and comments with relevant evidence, observations, and ideas. d) Acknowledge new information

expressed by others, and, when warranted, qualify or justify their own views in light of the evidence presented.

2. Analyze the purpose of information presented in diverse media and formats (e.g., visually, quantitatively, orally) and evaluate the motives (e.g., social, commercial, political) behind its presentation.

3. Delineate a speaker's argument and specific claims, evaluating the soundness of the reasoning and relevance and sufficiency of the evidence and identifying when irrelevant evidence is introduced.

Strategies for Comprehension and Collaboration, Grades 6–8

 Organize Investigation and Discussion Around a Specific Topic

Put an advanced ELL in charge of organizing a group for research and discussion of a particular topic related to the subject area you teach. The group leader assigns roles to each participant. Consider how the various group roles, such as recorder, editor, timekeeper, liaison, and so forth, might be better suited for students across a range of language levels. An early intermediate stage ELL could become frustrated being the recorder for the group but could contribute as timekeeper. An intermediate stage ELL could function fully as the group's liaison to the teacher and other groups because that job involves oral more than written communication. As stated in chapter 7, early advanced ELLs are well suited to be recorders for groups.

One of the duties of the group leader is to establish and ensure rules for the group. EdChange.org (edchange.org) suggests rules for successful group interaction (Figure 8.6).

Figure 8.6 Rules for Successful Group Interaction

1. Listen actively—respect others when they are talking.
2. Speak from your own experience instead of generalizing. Use *I* instead of *they*, *we*, and *you*.
3. Do not be afraid to respectfully challenge one another by asking questions, but refrain from personal attacks—focus on ideas.
4. Participate to the fullest of your ability—community growth depends on the inclusion of every individual voice.
5. Instead of invalidating somebody else's story with your own spin on her or his experience, share your own story and experience.
6. The goal is not to agree—it is to gain deeper understanding.
7. Be conscious of body language and nonverbal responses—they can be as disrespectful as words.

Source: http://www.edchange.org/multicultural/activities/groundrules.html

Produce, Write, and Narrate a Digital Story or Presentation

Early advanced ELLs can work collaboratively to contribute and narrate a script for a digital production. One way to push advanced ELLs into developing more complex language is to ask them to work individually or in small groups to produce, write, and narrate digital stories or presentations.

Organize the production
♦ Organize a group to create a digital production.
♦ Assign roles to each group member.
♦ Establish a project planner with tasks and due dates.
♦ Oversee the production.
♦ Edit the script.
♦ Edit the video or presentation software presentation.
♦ Present the completed work to the class.

Write the script
♦ Conceive of an idea or a concept for the production.
♦ Develop a storyboard to illustrate the sequence (see chapter 7).
♦ Write narration for each frame of the storyboard.
♦ Time each frame to coincide with the narration.

Narrate
♦ Participate in writing the script.
♦ Rehearse reading the narration for fluency and pacing in alignment with the video.
♦ Record the narration.
♦ Review and re-record as needed.

Lead a Vote with Your Feet Session

In the previous chapter, I discussed the voting with your feet activity as a means to conduct an analysis of a speaker's opinion or a written opinion in a text.

Figure 8.7 Sample Summary Table for Vote with Your Feet Positions

Agree	Undecided	Disagree

Early advanced ELLs can fully participate in the activity of taking a position, arguing their opinion, and trying to persuade others to share the same position; advanced ELLs can take on the role of teacher and be responsible for organizing and conducting the activity. The procedure is the same, but in this case, an advanced ELL is responsible for establishing the rules of the activity, monitoring pacing, and moderating the discussions.

The final part of the activity is leading the class in outlining the main points of a position. Using the table in Figure 8.7 (page 157), the class leader asks group members to summarize their positions of "Agree," "Undecided," or "Disagree."

Figure 8.8 Common Core State Standards for Listening and Speaking: Grades 9–12

Note: An English language learner at the level 5, advanced stage, can be expected to actively participate and excel in all standards. It may be easy to overlook that the student is still an English language learner at this level but linguistic and academic supports continue to be necessary.

Grades 9–10	1. Initiate and participate effectively in a range of collaborative discussions (one-on-one, in groups, and teacher-led) with diverse partners on *grades 9–10 topics, texts, and issues,* building on others' ideas and expressing their own clearly and persuasively. a) Come to discussions prepared, having read and researched material under study; explicitly draw on that preparation by referring to evidence from texts and other research on the topic or issue to stimulate a thoughtful, well-reasoned exchange of ideas. b) Work with peers to set rules for collegial discussions and decision-making (e.g., informal consensus, taking votes on key issues, presentation of alternate views), clear goals and deadlines, and individual roles as needed. c) Propel conversations by posing and responding to questions that relate the current discussion to broader themes or larger ideas; actively incorporate others into the discussion; and clarify, verify, or challenge ideas and conclusions. d) Respond thoughtfully to diverse perspectives, summarize points of agreement and disagreement, and, when warranted, qualify or justify their own views and understanding and make new connections in light of the evidence and reasoning presented. 2. Integrate multiple sources of information presented in diverse media or formats (e.g., visually, quantitatively, orally) evaluating the credibility and accuracy of each source. 3. Evaluate a speaker's point of view, reasoning, and use of evidence and rhetoric, identifying any fallacious reasoning or exaggerated or distorted evidence.
Grades 11–12	1. Initiate and participate effectively in a range of collaborative discussions (one-on-one, in groups, and teacher-led) with diverse partners on *grades 11–12 topics, texts, and issues,* building on others' ideas and expressing their own clearly

and persuasively. a) Come to discussions prepared, having read and researched material under study; explicitly draw on that preparation by referring to evidence from texts and other research on the topic or issue to stimulate a thoughtful, well-reasoned exchange of ideas. b) Work with peers to promote civil, democratic discussions and decision-making, set clear goals and deadlines, and establish individual roles as needed. c) Propel conversations by posing and responding to questions that probe reasoning and evidence; ensure a hearing for a full range of positions on a topic or issue; clarify, verify, or challenge ideas and conclusions; and promote divergent and creative perspectives. d) Respond thoughtfully to diverse perspectives; synthesize comments, claims, and evidence made on all sides of an issue; resolve contradictions when possible; and determine what additional information or research is required to deepen the investigation or complete the task.

2. Integrate multiple sources of information presented in diverse formats and media (e.g., visually, quantitatively, orally) in order to make informed decisions and solve problems, evaluating the credibility and accuracy of each source and noting any discrepancies among the data.

3. Evaluate a speaker's point of view, reasoning, and use of evidence and rhetoric, assessing the stance, premises, links among ideas, word choice, points of emphasis, and tone used.

Strategies for Comprehension and Collaboration, Grades 9–12

Take the Lead with a Group Problem Solving Project and Presentation

Advanced ELLs are in a position to take on leadership roles with group projects. As called for by the standards, they could be responsible for bringing a group to consensus about the goals, objectives, and approach to the project. A project-planning tool such as the planner in Figure 8.9 (page 160) can help organize the project. Developing the planner will also facilitate discussion about the project in terms of identifying the overarching goal(s) and objectives or tasks that must be completed to do the project.

Write and Present an Abstract of a Research Study

There are many directions to follow in response to the standards. I selected the task of writing an abstract for a research article because the action involves higher-level thinking and language use. The difference between what an advanced ELL would do with this exercise and what would be required from an early advanced ELL is that the advanced ELL can reasonably be expected to complete the task on his or her own. The task, therefore, would include selecting

Figure 8.9 Project Planner and Organizer

Project Title		
Goal(s)		
Objective/Task 1	Who is responsible?	Due Completed? Y/N
Objective/Task 2	Who is responsible?	Due Completed? Y/N
Objective/Task 3	Who is responsible?	Due Completed? Y/N
Objective/Task 4	Who is responsible?	Due Completed? Y/N

Source: Created by the author.

an appropriate research article, reading it for understanding, abstracting the major components, and presenting the abstraction to the rest of the class. The work sheet in Figure 8.10 on the next page facilitates writing a 300-word abstract that could be presented as a single paragraph, in the form of a research poster, or in a media format using presentation software.

Lead a Small-Group Discussion Following a Speaker's Presentation on a Topic

Advanced stage ELLs should have opportunities to lead discussion groups. To meet the requirements of the standard, the leader guides the small-group discussion through a series of evaluations of a speaker's presentation. Those areas of evaluation include "point of view, reasoning, and use of evidence and rhetoric, assessing the stance, premises, links among ideas, word choice, points of emphasis, and tone used" (Common Core Listening and Speaking, Comprehension and Collaboration, Standard 3). The items to evaluate appear in no particular order in this standard, which adds to the complexity of the task of leading a discussion.

To evaluate one or more of the items listed in the standard, the leader must not only understand each of those terms but also conceive of appropriate questions, respond to participants, moderate the pacing and tone of the discussion, ensure that the group stays on topic, and synthesize what the group members said. This high level of functioning in English can be facilitated with a framework that organizes the categories of evaluation into rhetoric and reasoning and provides reminders of what each term means (Figure 8.11, page 162). The organizing frame can also be used for taking notes during discussion.

Figure 8.10 300-Word Research Abstract Work Sheet

Sentence Prompts
1. Write a sentence or more in each box below according to the prompts provided.
2. Keep the number of words within the suggested range provided for each category.
3. Compile the sentences into a 300-word abstract.
4. Title the abstract with the name of the research project.
5. Present the abstract as a paragraph, poster, or media presentation.

Problem: Begin with a statement of the problem or topic addressed by the research.	*(40–50 words)*
Context: State the context of the research. • *What* is the theoretical background? • *Who* are the action researchers? • *Where*? Location • *Who*? Participant information (number, gender, ethnicity, socio-economic status)	*(50–70 words)*
Methodology: Briefly describe the methodology of the study. • Cite source for methodology. • State the basic steps of the research study.	*(30–60 words)*
Findings: Summarize the principal findings. • Order findings according to the research questions. • Keep it to major findings. • Avoid listing every finding.	*(50–70 words)*
Conclusions: Summarize: • Major conclusions • Recommendations for practice • Recommendations for additional research	*(30–50 words)*

Source: Adapted from Richard Sagor, *The Action Research Guidebook: A Four-Step Process for Educators and School Teams* (Thousand Oaks, CA: Corwin Press, 2005) 163. Print.

Figure 8.11 Organizing Frame for Evaluating a Speaker's Presentation

Rhetoric		Reasoning	
Stance	Objective? Subjective?	**Point of view**	Whose perspective?
Word choice	Contributes to or detracts from the argument	**Premises**	Foundations of the argument
Points of emphasis	What's important? How did you know?	**Use of evidence**	Valid arguments?
Tone	Formal? Informal? Serious? Humorous? Ironic? Condescending? Other?	**Links among ideas**	Identify connections

Source: Created by the author.

References

Afflerbach, P., & Clark, S. (2011). Diversity and English language arts assessment. In D. Lapp and D. Fisher (Eds.), *Handbook of research on teaching the English language arts* (3rd ed.) (pp. 307–313). New York, NY: Routledge.

Asher, J. (1969). The total physical response approach to second language learning. *The Modern Language Journal, 53*(1), 3–17.

Asher, J., Kusudo, J., & de la Torre, R. (1974). Learning a second language through commands: The second field test. *Modern Language Journal, 58*(2), 24–32.

August, D., & Shanahan, T. (2007). Developing literacy in second language learners. The report of the National Literacy Panel. Santa Cruz, CA: Center for Applied Linguistics.

August, D., Carlo, M., Dressler, C., & Snow, C. (2005). The critical role of vocabulary development for English language learners. *Learning Disabilities Research & Practice, 20*(1), 50–55.

Bear, D.R., Invernizzi, M., Templeton, S., & Johnston, F. (2000). *Words their way: Word study for phonics, vocabulary, and spelling instruction* (2nd ed.). Upper Saddle. River, NJ: Prentice Hall.

Boyd-Batstone, P. (2006). *Differentiated early literacy for English language learners.* Boston, MA: Allyn & Bacon.

Burgstahler, Sheryl, & Cory, Rebecca. (2008). *Universal Design in Higher Education: From Principles to Practice.* Cambridge, MA: Harvard Education Press.

Bruner, J. (1972). *Actual minds, possible worlds.* Boston, MA: Harvard Press.

Butler, F. A., Lord, C., Stevens, R., Borrego, M., & Bailey, A. L. (2003/2004). *An approach to operationalizing academic language for language test development purposes: Evidence from fifth-grade science and math* (IES, Contract No. R305B960002). (CSE Tech. Rep. No. 626). Los Angeles, CA: University of California, National Center for Research on Evaluation, Standards, and Student Testing.

Carlo, M., August, D., McLaughlin, B., Snow, C., Dressler, C., Lippman, D., . . . & White, C. (2004). Closing the gap: Addressing the vocabulary needs of English-language learners in bilingual and mainstream classrooms. *Reading Research Quarterly, 39*(2) 188–215.

Collier, V., & Thomas, W. (1987). How quickly can immigrants become proficient in school English? *The Journal of Educational Issues of Language Minority Students, 5,* 26–38.

Common Core State Standards. http://db.readinglions.net/commoncore/index.lasso?fa=search.

Cox, C., & Many, J. (1992). Toward an understanding of the aesthetic response to literature. *Language Arts, 69*(1), 28–33.

Cube image. Retrieved from http://en.wikipedia.org/wiki/Cube.

Cummins, J. (2000). *Language power and pedagogy*. Tonawanda, NY: UTP.

Cummins, J. (2001). Empowering minority students: A framework for intervention. *Harvard Educational Review, 7*(4), 649–676.

Douglas Gould and Company (2004). Writing a media analysis. Retrieved from www.ccmc.org/sites/default/files/WorkingPaper2.pdf.

Dutro, S. (2008). *A focused approach to systematic ELD handbook*. San Clemente, CA: E.L. Achieve. (www.elachieve.org) (The Express Placement Assessment is included in the handbook.)

Federal Interagency Forum on Child and Family Statistics. (2009). *America's children: Key national indicators of well-being, 2009*. Washington, DC: U.S. Government Printing Office.

Fitzgerald, J., & Noblit, G. (2000). Balance in the making: learning to read in an ethnically diverse first grade classroom. *Journal of Educational Psychology, 92*(1), 3–22.

Gentry, R. (1996). *My Kid can't spell: Understanding and assisting your child's literacy development*. Portsmouth, NH: Heinemann.

Graham, C. (2000). *Jazz chants*. ESL.net (http://www.esl.net/jazz_chants.htm.)

Graham, T. (2002). *Disarmament sketches: Three decades of arms control and international law*. Seattle, WA: University of Washington Press.

I don't know. (n.d.). In Google Images. Retrieved from http://www.google.com/search?tbm=isch&hl=en&source=hp&biw=1203&bih=618&q=I+don%27t+know&gbv=2&oq=I+don%27t+know&aq=f&aqi=g10&aql=&gs_l=img.3..0l10.2303l5497l0l7526l12l12l0l5l5l0l66l382l7l7l0.frgbld.#q=I+don%27t+know&hl=en&gbv=2&tbm=isch&bav=on.2,or.r_gc.r_pw.r_qf.,cf.osb&fp=6012509dede775aa&biw=1061&bih=586.

Koelsch, N., Walqui, A., Hamburger, L., Gaarder, D, Insaurralde, A., Schmida, M., . . . Estrada, P. (2010). *What are we doing to middle school English learners? Findings and recommendations for change from a study of California EL programs (research report)*. San Francisco, CA: WestEd.

Krashen, S., & Terrell, T. (1984). *The natural approach: Language acquisition in the classroom*. Hayward, CA: Alemany Press.

Larson, L., Boyd-Batstone, P., & Cox, C. (2009). What is a quality on-line discussion posting? Testing the inter-rater reliability of discourse function rubric of on-line video case study (OVCS) discussion posted by pre-service teachers on-line discussion posting. In J. Salmons and L. Wilson (Eds.), *Handbook of research on electronic collaboration and organizational synergy* (pp. 387-398). Hershey, PA: Information Science Reference.

LeGuillou, J. P. (2011). *Pathways to prosperity: Meeting the challenge of preparing young people for the 21st century*. Boston, MA: Harvard Graduate School of Education.

Lloyd, K. (June 25, 2012). Karen J. Lloyd's storyboard blog. Retrieved from karenjlloyd.com/blog/free-storyboard-template-downloads.

Mengpengyue. (2010, March 23). Toilet signs—male? female? Retrieved from hi.nciku.com/space.php?uid=31&do=blog&id=2732.

Moll, L., & Gonzalez, N. (1994). Lessons from research with language minority children. *Journal of Reading Behavior*, 26(4), 23–41.

Moskowitz, J., Malvin, J., Schaeffer, G., & Schaps, E. (1983). Evaluation of a cooperative learning strategy. *American Educational Research Journal*, 20, 687–696.

Murphy, A., Bailey, A., & Butler, F. (2006). *California English language development standards & assessment: Evaluating linkage & alignment*. www.cde.ca.gov/ta/tg/el/documents/linkagealignstudy.pdf.

No Child Left Behind (2001a). *No child left behind, title III: Language instruction for limited English proficient and immigrant students*. Washington, DC: George Washington University, National Clearinghouse for Bilingual Education.

No Child Left Behind (2001b). *No child left behind, title I: Improving the academic achievement of the disadvantaged*. 107th Congress, 1st session, December 13, 2001. Washington, DC: George Washington University, National Clearinghouse for Bilingual Education.

Olsen, L. (2010). *Reparable harm: Fulfilling the unkept promise of educational opportunities for California's long-term English learners*. Long Beach, CA: Californians Together. Retrieved from http://www.sccoe.org/depts/ell/bcn/Sep2010/BCN%209-16-10/12a_Reparable%20Harm%20Long%20Term%20ELs-CA%20PDF.pdf.

Paris, D., & Ball, A. F. (2009). Teacher knowledge in culturally and linguistically complex classrooms: Lessons from the Golden Age and beyond. In L. Mandel Morrow, R. Rueda, and D. Lapp (Eds.), *Handbook of research on literacy and diversity* (pp. 379–395). New York, NY: Guilford Press.

Predictable-pattern books: literacy.kent.edu/Oasis/Pubs/patterns.html.

Purcell-Gates, V. (2004). *Developing print literacy: Cognitive and social theory*. Boston, MA: Harvard Press.

Sacramento (1999). *California English language development standards*. California Department of Education. http://www.cde.ca.gov/be/st/ss/documents/englangdevstnd.pdf.

Sadler, (1989). Formative assessment and the design of instructional systems. *Instructional Science*, 13, 191–209.

Sagor, R. (2005). *The action research guidebook: A four-step process for educators and school teams*. Thousand Oaks, CA: Corwin Press.

Sato, E., Lagunoff, R., Worth, P., Bailey A. L., & Butler, F. A. (2005). *ELD standards linkage and test alignment under title III: A pilot study of the CELDT and the California ELD and content standards*. Final report (June) to the California Department of Education, Sacramento, CA.

Schifini, A. (1985). *Sheltered English: Content area instruction for limited English proficient students*. Los Angeles, CA: Los Angeles County Office of Education.

Shin, F., & Krashen, S. (2007). *Summer reading: Program and evidence*. Boston, MA: Allyn & Bacon/Pearson Education.

Slavin, R. E. (2011). Instruction based on cooperative learning. In R. Mayer (Ed.), *Handbook of research on learning and instruction*. London, UK: Taylor & Francis.

Sobol, D. (1995). Specially designed academic instruction in English. ERIC (ED 391357.)

Teacher Vision printable templates. http://www.teachervision.fen.com/graphic-organizers/printable/48390.html.

TESOL Standards K–12. Retrieved from http://www2.gisd.k12.nm.us/standards/esl/index.html.

Valdez, V. E., & Callahan, R. M. (2011). Who is learning language(s) in today's schools? In D. Lapp and D. Fisher (Eds.), *Handbook of research on teaching the English language arts* (3rd ed.) (pp. 3–9). New York, NY: Routledge.

Vogt, M. E., Echevarria, J., & Short, D. (2004, 2007). *Making content comprehensible for English learners: The SIOP model*. Boston, MA: Allyn & Bacon/Pearson Education.

Vygotsky, L. (1996). *Thought and language* (9th ed.). Cambridge, MA: MIT Press.

World-Class Instructional Design and Assessment (WIDA) (2012). ELD Standards. http://www.wida.us/standards/eld.aspx.

Xu, S.H. (2010). *Teaching English language learners: Literacy strategies and resources for K–6*. New York, NY: Guilford Press.

Yancy, K. B. (2009). *Writing for the 21st Century*. National Council of Teachers of English. ERIC: ED504396.